Love and Logic Magic
for
Lasting Relationships

Jim Fay and Dr. David B. Hawkins

Love and Logic Magic for Lasting Relationships

Jim Fay and Dr. David B. Hawkins

www.loveandlogic.com
800-338-4065

Love and Logic Institute, Inc.
2207 Jackson St
Golden, CO 80401
www.loveandlogic.com
800-338-4065

Love and Logic, Love & Logic, Becoming a Love and Logic Parent, America's Parenting Experts, Love and Logic Magic, 9 Essential Skills for the Love and Logic Classroom, LOVE AND LOGIC EARLY CHILDHOOD PARENTING MADE FUN!, EARLY CHILDHOOD PARENTING MADE FUN! and <heart logo> are registered trademarks or trademarks of the Institute For Professional Development, Ltd. and may not be used without written permission expressly granted from the Institute For Professional Development, Ltd.

ISBN# 978-1-935326-07-6

Library of Congress Cataloging-in-Publication Data

Fay, Jim.
  Love and logic magic for lasting relationships / by Jim Fay and David Hawkins.
      p. cm.
  Includes index.
  ISBN 978-1-935326-07-6
  1. Interpersonal relations--Psychological aspects. 2. Interpersonal conflict. 3. Interpersonal communication. I. Hawkins, David. II. Title.
  BF636.F35 2011
  158.2--dc22

                          2011007248

Editor: Christie Hawkins
Cover & Book Design: Michael Snell, Shade of the Cottonwood, Lawrence, KS
Project Coordinator: Kelly Borden

 Published and printed in the United States of America

Table of Contents

Preface

I thought I recognized the name on the email, Dr. David Hawkins, and then it hit me. "Yes," I thought. "This guy is the famous Relationship Doctor. I know about his work and his books. He is the director of the famous Marriage Recovery Center." His email said that he had a proposal for me. That tweaked my interest so I got on the phone with him.

Dr. Hawkins told me about his practice and how it had evolved over the years. "Jim," he said, "I had been an effective counselor for a number of years. Regardless of my success, I was always looking for more effective techniques that would give my clients the confidence and resolve it takes to repair and maintain their relationships.

"I became acquainted with the *Love and Logic* principals and started blending them with my own techniques. The result has been so rewarding that it's time for us to write a book together. Just think, Jim. You and my wife, Christie, and I can collaborate to turn out a book that can change the world of relationship building in the same way that the *Love and Logic* principals have changed the world of parenting."

I was honored and excited until I thought, "Wait a minute. David and Christie live in the great Northwest. I live in Golden,

Colorado. That's at least 1500 miles away. The actual mechanics of two writers, working in the same room, producing a book are exhausting enough. How are we going to do this from different parts of the country? The logistics seemed overwhelming."

The whole challenge was intriguing enough that we arranged to spend several days together, discussing the concepts and mapping out the book. We decided that modern technology could solve many of the logistical and mechanical problems. But one big problem still remained.

The problem had to do with the voice of the book. How do you blend the voices of three people in a way that doesn't confuse readers or cause the reading to become cumbersome?

We finally decided that David would become the voice of the book. I would provide the *Love and Logic* conceptual and technical expertise, and Christie would be the one to edit, referee the relationship, and keep the two guys on the straight and narrow.

It turned out to be a delightful experience for the three of us. Some of the writing was done in Golden, Colorado. Some was produced in Seattle, Washington, while the rest was created on the beaches of sunny Todos Santos, Mexico. Then modern technology worked its magic, blending the experience and wisdom of three new friends into what you are about to read. It is the fusion of the *Love and Logic* way and expertise of Dr. David Hawkins.

Enjoy,

Jim Fay
Co-founder of the Love and Logic Institute, Inc.

Prologue

"Don't turn away from possible futures before you're certain you don't have anything to learn from them. You're always free to change your mind and choose a different future, or a different past."

—Richard Bach

The Wisdom of *Love and Logic*

The brilliant information in the following pages is born out of years of research and positive results by the masters of the *Love and Logic* approach. This program and best-selling book, co-authored by Jim Fay and Dr. Foster Cline, are used in thousands of schools across the nation and in hundreds of thousands of homes. These are tried and true principles used to raise healthy and happy children.

The *Love and Logic* approach is the foundation for this book and has helped millions of people raise wonderful, healthy children. Now we're taking all that wisdom which works so well with kids, and applying it to adult relationships. As sure as peanut butter and jelly were meant to be together, *Love and Logic* principles were meant to be adapted to adult relationships. Here, in *Love and Logic Magic for Lasting Relationships*, the authors share *Love and Logic* techniques that can easily be used to create fun, lively, loving relationships in your adult world.

The *Love and Logic* Way

I first became familiar with the *Love and Logic* approach at least fifteen years ago. At the time I was a professional psychologist and the father of two adolescent sons, Joshua and Tyson. Imagine my incredible frustration at being an educated man, trained in the field of psychology, knowing about behavior modification and other tools, and still feeling completely helpless at navigating the troubled waters of rearing two disrespectful (and did I mention rebellious?) boys.

I was supposed to have the answers. I studied every program known to man—behavior modification, corporal punishment, encouragement—I tried them all. Each fell short of being comprehensive, understandable, simple or doable.

And then I stumbled upon this approach. My friend Jerry, a ninth grade school teacher, invited me to a conference on "child discipline." Anxious to help my sons get along with one another, as well as with me and their mother, I signed up.

What happened over the next several weeks was nothing short of amazing.

Watching and discussing a series of videos by Jim Fay, nationally renowned educator, and Foster Cline, M.D., child specialist and psychiatrist, bowled me over.

First, *training and disciplining kids could be easy.* They shared how too many parents are simply working too hard. Keeping up with complicated systems of charts, graphs, stars and stickers, was difficult. Parents were doing too much of the work.

"Let the kids do more of the thinking and work," Fay and Cline advised.

That sure made sense.

Second, *parenting should be fun.* Fun! These guys really got my

attention with that one. How in the world could I have fun trying to get my kids to pick up their dirty clothes? How could I have
fun getting them to quit bickering with one another? How in the
world could I have fun getting them to treat me with respect?

Third, *every principle taught was logical*. No fancy gimmicks. No
rocket-science trickery. Plain, simple, logical tools.

"This is too simple," I said at first, until I began experimenting
and getting positive results.

Finally, these educators suggested *you can remain calm and teach
using empathy*. I have to admit that when I heard this, I was skepti-
cal. My oldest son, Joshua, was just hitting his stride as a willful
teenager. My staying calm seemed impossible, when his emotions
were as volatile as dynamite.

During the next ten weeks I learned and experimented with
many techniques that were both *loving and logical*. They were easily
learned, fun and *they worked!* They worked!

"Amazing," I thought. "These principles are based upon using
empathy, treating each other with dignity and respect, and developing clear boundaries. I agree with everything."

My sons soon became guinea pigs for my latest (of many!)
psychological experiments. Heaven knows they'd been analyzed,
therapized and modified. But having discovered the *Love and Logic*
approach, I felt that I was no longer coming to the end of the
road, but was facing the beginning of a new journey.

My boys thrived under this program, and I soon found what
millions of parents already knew—this stuff works! No sooner had
I begun using these principles with my sons than I began teaching
other parents. I couldn't keep it a secret.

Four Basic Principals of *Love and Logic*

Finding incredible success with these principles, and with a nation buzzing about this *Love and Logic* stuff, I began thinking more
about these principles.

Jim Fay and Foster Cline promoted Four Basic Tenets that are
so—well, logical. I wondered why I hadn't discovered them before

hearing about these two guys from Colorado. They say that everything flows out of four important principles:

1. **We always maintain the dignity of individuals:** Everyone desires to be treated with dignity. There is never a need to shame or disrespect another person.

2. **We share control:** We share control over how we're going to solve problems. We understand that you control your feelings and actions, I control my feelings and actions, and we control our relationship. Control is such a strong basic need that the more we share the more we get back.

3. **We share the thinking:** It is up to us to think about our problems. We negotiate with one another over the direction of our relationship. Asking for another's thoughts provides dignity, enhances relationships, and shares control.

4. **We follow an empathy/consequence formula:** We work together to develop healthy boundaries, and understand that empathy is the glue that holds us together. Providing empathy for others' problems instead of telling them what to do provides dignity, shares the thinking, shares control, and enhances relationships.

Not only does the *Love and Logic* approach work, but it is built upon powerful principles. This stuff would stand up to the scrutiny of Sigmund Freud if he were still alive.

Actually, through discussions with Jim Fay, I discovered that Fay was strongly influenced by Abraham Maslow, the renowned psychologist who developed *The Hierarchy of Human Needs*, still widely accepted today. Using Maslov as a guide, Fay and Cline defined the four basic human needs as:

The importance of physical and emotional safety.
The importance of love and affection.
The importance of healthy control.
The importance of being needed.

They determined that when these needs were met for a child in the family, the child developed into a healthy and loving adult. When these are not violated in adult relationships, relationships blossom.

Love and Logic with Adults

Four basic human needs: creating physical and emotional safety, giving and receiving love and affection, maintaining healthy control, and feeling needed. If these principles created healthy adults out of children, doesn't it make sense that they would work in adult relationships, creating healthy and loving adults out of adults?

Not willing to leave well enough alone, and after years of these principles oozing into my pores, I had one of those *Eureka!* experiences, when you know that coffee and frothed milk could create something magical, if not slightly addicting.

About a year ago, I was sitting in my office with a thirty-something couple, listening to them arguing about how to raise their children.

Susan, a no-nonsense businesswoman, stared at her husband, Tyler, and bluntly told him everything he was doing with their two daughters was wrong.

"You let them get away with everything," she accused.

Tyler countered defensively, "I'm just not all over them the way you are. You nit-pick everything they say and do."

"That is absolutely not true," Susan's voice escalated as she glared at Tyler. "I need you to back me when I discipline the girls."

"What if I don't agree with the way you discipline them? What if I think they respond better to love, clear boundaries, and no yelling?"

"Doesn't that sound ideal," Susan sarcastically replied, "but you are so inconsistent."

I felt my energy drain. Racking my brain for tools and techniques to offer them, I introduced the *Love and Logic* approach. Abandoning their fight, they became excited, listening as I talked about a program that could help them with their children.

In the middle of talking to them about these concepts however, I had my *Eurkea!* moment. *Love and Logic. It's not just for kids!*

Could it be possible to not only practice *Love and Logic* in their parenting, but also in their personal relationship?

Could the *Love and Logic* principals apply to adult relationships?

I decided to give it a try. It was like introducing peanut butter to jelly and frothed milk to coffee. This had to be what Edison felt when he invented the electric light bulb. Why hadn't someone combined these principles sooner?

Love and Logic Tools with Adults

I began an experiment. Over the next few months I worked with Susan and Tyler, asking them to put on a playful, experimental attitude. I asked them to forget what they'd previously been taught about relating, and consider a new way of interacting with one another.

I gave them this speech:

"What if relating did not need to be such grueling work? What if I could teach you some new techniques and principles, which take the work out of relating and create loving growing relationships? Would you be interested? You must understand that you will screw up royally. But that's good, that's what I want. When you do screw up, all I ask is that you notice what happened, because *mistakes are great opportunities for learning.*"

"Do you have an open mind for practicing new principles? There will be four principles at the heart of everything we do: *maintaining dignity in every interaction, sharing control, sharing thinking, and having empathy and consequences in your relating.*"

They readily agreed with these principles.

"Over the next nine weeks we'll experiment with nine different tools, which you can use in parenting your daughters. And there's a bonus. What if I promised that not only will they work with your kids, but they will work on your colleagues and each other too? Are you in? This stuff is dynamite," I said smiling. "It'll shake things up and create a relationship like you've never known."

"Let's do it," they answered in unison. "When do we start?"

"Well, let's just look at a summary of our tools, and then flesh them out over the next nine weeks."

Neutralizing Arguments: You'll learn how to end those nasty power struggles. No more blow-ups, escalations, stomping out of the room episodes. I hope you're not too attached to them, because they've got to go.

Delaying Consequences: You'll learn to slow things down, think things over, and use consequences effectively in your relationships.

Unleashing the Power of Empathy: You'll learn how empathy binds our hearts to our kids, mates and those we care about. Empathy is the bridge that keeps us attached to others.

Setting Limits with Enforceable Consequences: You'll learn how this is so powerful with kids, but can also be used with adults. You'll learn the power of sharing remorse, taking responsibility as well as making amends for actions.

Guiding Others to Solve Their Own Problems: You'll learn how to let go of rescuing. You'll learn to solve many of your own problems while having empathy for others, thereby releasing them to solve their own problems.

Creating Strategic Planning Sessions: You'll learn how to have regular Strategic Planning Sessions with those you care about, whether with your children, your mate or adult friends. You'll learn how to monitor growth, make good use out of mistakes and have fun in the process.

Sharing the Load: You'll learn how to work cooperatively with each other. Like an Indianapolis 500 Race Team, you and your mate will learn to work cooperatively, sharing the work and love load. You'll learn to meet each other's needs enabling the "team" to work efficiently.

Offering Choices within Limits: You'll learn how to offer choices within limits. You'll learn to create an environment in which you can be safe and grow, and your love life can blossom.

Catching Them Doing It Right: You'll learn the importance of catching your mate doing the things you love. Positive feedback and utter admiration make the world go around—not to mention make your mate try harder to please you.

"Again, this stuff is dynamite," I said to Susan and Tyler. "We're going to have a blast (no pun intended) trying these out. You might find one or two that are uniquely suited for your relationship, and chuck the rest out the window. That's okay. This is a new recipe, and you are the cooks. And there's room for two cooks in this kitchen! Are you ready for an experiment?"

I worked with Susan and Tyler over the next nine weeks. They loved the material, though they made plenty of mistakes. They came to see their mistakes as opportunities, rather than failures. They became excited about using the "recipe," referring back to it when they made mistakes, becoming, over time, more efficient and effective in their relating.

We Love Mistakes

Many of these skills may seem foreign to you. Just as you entered parenting without a training manual, you also entered adult relationships unsure of what to expect. Like me, you've stumbled along, unsure of the mistakes you were making, but recognized you were making them.

Rather than being threatened by mistakes, we want you to embrace them. Making mistakes means you've got a learning opportunity sitting in front of you. Rather than dreading your relationship problems, we want you to embrace them. Every problem has a solution.

Can you give yourself permission to practice without perfection? Can you have fun along the way? We're still learning new tools and ways to use the powerful *Love and Logic* material, but we know that these tools will work for you.

When you mess up, and you will, we want you to smile. Yes, smile. We want you to talk to your mate ahead of time and make this agreement:

"We are learning some new techniques. Like learning anything else, we'll probably take two steps forward, and one back. On some days, we will take one step forward and two steps back. We're going to make mistakes. That is natural and to be expected. When we do, we'll forgive each other. Over time, we'll notice our progress. **And we have to have fun.** If it's not fun, we're not doing it!"

Okay. The pressure is now off. Ready to make mistakes, you'll move forward, trying out new techniques, finding which ones work best for you. You're also going to have fun along the way.

Five Second Experiments

Finally, you'll notice many opportunities throughout the book to experiment. We love experiments! With a willingness to fail, we'll ask you to try out a new behavior. Again, this requires a playful attitude. You're going to stay loose, let go of previous ways of behaving, and give the new technique a try. The beauty of an experiment is that there is no commitment. If you don't like the results, go on to another experiment or go back to your old ways.

Some of these experiments will be colossal failures. Complete, total, miserable failures. You'll look at one another and wonder why you agreed to try the experiment. Maybe you can adapt a technique or principle to your situation by asking each other how the experiment is working, or what needs to change. As with the invention of the electric light bulb, every failure brings you closer to success.

Other experiments will be incredible *Eureka!* moments. You will have discovered electricity, for the second time. You'll look at each other like you're sheer geniuses. Delight in your new discovery and add it to a growing list of tools and techniques that will lead you into the Promise Land.

Let's Get Going on Getting Along

We all want to get along. We all want a relationship free from conflict, filled with love. Are you tired of doing what you've always done, and getting what you've always gotten? Are you ready to have some fun and try some new techniques in your relationships?

Well then, you're on a fabulous path to getting along with others in your life—family, friends and mate. These techniques are powerful. Like Edison, you're working with electricity. No, you're playing with electricity, but we're sure you're safe and you're going to notice success in every relationship. This electricity is going to light up your life.

With a playful attitude and a curious spirit, let's get going with getting along. We've got a power-packed book waiting for you.

1

Neutralizing Arguments

I argue very well. Ask any of my remaining friends. I can win an argument on any topic, against any opponent. People know this, and steer clear of me at parties. Often, as a sign of their great respect, they don't even invite me."

—Dave Barry

"I was there last year," my Aunt Betty said during a family gathering. My cousin, Rick, was sharing about the great trip to the Grand Canyon he'd just returned from. "The Canyon isn't really as deep as some people think," Aunt Betty added, citing various facts.

"Hmm," he said. "I don't think you've got your facts straight."

"Oh, I know what I'm talking about," she persisted. My cousin became increasingly deflated and began to withdraw into silence.

Looking away, not wanting to get pulled into this discussion, I focused my attention on my sister, who was involved in another discussion with another cousin.

"You shouldn't put your kids in private school," my cousin, Sydney, asserted to my sister, a strong proponent of public education.

"Why not?" she asked.

"Oh, it's never as good as public education," my cousin said. "Inferior teachers. No sports program. Poor funding. The list goes on and on."

"But, there are lots of positives," my sister said. "Our kids get more attention and personal instruction."

"That's rubbish," my cousin said more heatedly. "You really need to rethink what you're doing. The impact on your kids future is incredible."

They continued to argue; again I decided not to get entangled in this conversation. Instead, I moved across the room. I hadn't gone more than a few steps when I heard my uncle talking sternly to his daughter.

"You need to move up in your department," he said. "If you don't make your move soon, you'll be passed over and never advance."

"I know what I'm doing, Dad," she responded defensively.

"Well," he countered, "I'm never sure you really do know what you're doing."

"Dad," she firmly replied, "I know what I'm doing. You don't need to tell me how to live my life."

"I'm not trying to tell you how to live your life. But obviously you could stand a little advice here and there."

"I'm doing fine, Dad," she said angrily and walked away.

I stood back and reflected upon what I was seeing—the frequency with which people argue—good people, loving people, friends and family engaged in petty arguments, serious arguments, divisive arguments, and all needless arguments.

Thankfully, this arguing is all unnecessary. While we may have tension with people, we don't need to experience undue friction. We don't need to live in a world of conflict, tension and arguments—in fact, we can all get along! Our first step in learning to get along is using this power tool: neutralizing arguments.

What if I could show you a way to powerfully end arguments with family, friends, and spouse before they begin? What if you became so adept at anticipating arguments, you saw them coming from a mile away and could choose, with time to spare, how you wanted to handle the situation—without conflict?

As much as we say we hate arguing, most of us do it with regularity. We've watched our parents and children fight, and we, too, slip easily into fighting. Sometimes it seems we embrace our fighting style, in spite of the tremendous damage it causes.

But, what if there is another way? What if there is a way to engage in lively conversation without bickering or arguing, accepting our differences and embracing opposing points of view? Would you be interested? What if you could disagree with your mate, your friends, your boss and still not argue?

There is another way! There is a tool so powerful you'll wish you'd learned it years ago. You're going to look back and see where this tool could have cut through years of conflict, maybe even saving broken friendships and increasing opportunities. The folks at the *Love and Logic* Institute gave us many powerful tools to change our relationships, and neutralizing arguments is one of them.

The Department Store

Arguing seems to be everywhere! The destructive power of arguing became quite apparent to me during an interaction with a clerk at a local department store. Having made a routine purchase of a pair of jeans, I got home to discover they were defective. (No, most men do not try on clothes at the store.) Well, no big deal. I would simply return them, exchanging them for a new pair.

Arriving at the store, I went straight to the Men's Department. The clerk was busy with paper work and barely glanced up when I arrived at the counter. I waited a few moments, beginning to bristle with annoyance.

"Excuse me," I said politely. "I'd like to exchange my jeans."

"I'll be with you in a moment," she said, continuing with her paperwork.

Waiting a few more moments, which seemed like hours, I again interrupted her.

"Can you help me?" I asked impatiently.

"I need to finish this and it might be a few more minutes," she said. "Maybe you can go over to another register," she said, pointing to the Women's Department.

"I just want to exchange some jeans," I said, growing more irritated. "It should just take a moment."

"If you go over there, someone will be able to help you," she said curtly. "I said I can't help you right now. They will help you in the Women's Department."

"But I just want to exchange a pair of jeans," I repeated. "It will take you two minutes!"

"I can't help you now," she continued. "I need to complete something and my register is closed. Go over to the checkout in the Women's Department."

"I want to talk to your manager," I blurted. "This is crazy!"

"She's not here," the woman said angrily, "and I'm the Department Manager. I told you I cannot help you right now, but they can help you in the Women's Department."

Furious, I grabbed my jeans and headed out the door. Fuming for the next twenty minutes, I had just experienced the destructive power of arguing. What had it gotten me? I was now unhappy and I still had to return my jeans.

Conflicts in Marriage

The destructive power of arguing, and our need for a tool like neutralizing arguments, again became apparent to me the following day during an emergency marriage session. Karen called and asked if I could work her and husband, Cole, into my schedule. She sounded desperate.

"I've been telling Cole for years that I don't feel loved in our marriage," Karen began, eyes filling with tears.

"Crazy," he began. "I work hard to provide for you."

"Fine," she blurted. "You provide nicely. I have every thing I need, but I still don't feel loved."

"What do you think is missing, Karen?" I interrupted.

"Time where he just listens to what is going on in my life."

"I do that," Cole protested. "Last night I sat on the couch with you for half an hour and listened to you complain about your mother. Isn't that a sign of love?"

"But, you weren't really listening," she said. "You had one eye on me and one on the football game."

I watched Cole stare at Karen, withdrawing into a cold silence.

I asked Karen to stop for a moment while I checked in with Cole.

"Cole, how are you feeling about what Karen is saying?" I asked.

"I'm trying to listen, but everything I say turns into a fight. Then if I just listen and don't reply, she gets mad and we get into a fight because she says I'm not listening."

"Karen," I said, "you are nursing a lot of wounds from things Cole has done and said. Is that right?"

"More than we can talk about in one day," Karen retorted, glaring at Cole.

"Well I have a lot of complaints, too," Cole interjected forcefully. "It's not just about you. I don't like the way things are going either. You act like it's just your feelings that are hurt. You are always the victim. I have my own list of complaints you know, but there's no use sharing them. You can't hear me."

"I've always listened to you," Karen said angrily. "I can't believe you are pointing the finger at me. You're just saying that because of my complaints about you."

"See what I mean?" Cole said, looking to me. "I can't talk about my concerns. It's all about her."

"I know we've got a bunch of issues to talk about," I said, trying to stave off more arguing. "Past hurts, feelings of betrayal, and neither of you feeling understood. I think I know where you're coming from."

I took a moment to let my words sink in.

"You want to make your mate understand how hurt you are. You each want the other to care about your feelings. Would you be interested in learning about a tool that will help end these battles?"

"Yes," they said in unison.

"OK," I again paused, knowing this tool would unlock their power struggles. I knew the tool of neutralizing arguments has the power of revolutionizing their relationship (and perhaps yours too). It has the power to change how you interact with your mate, your family, your workmates and even store clerks.

"But, before I teach you this most powerful tool," I continued, "you must understand why things go south for so many people."

Fruitless Arguing

"Why do you think you argue?" I asked Karen and Cole.

"We want to be heard," Karen answered.

"Is that all?"

"We want to be understood," Cole answered.

"You're both right," I said. "We all want to be listened to, understood and have our feelings validated. We want those in our life to take in what we're saying and be influenced by it."

"Imagine," I continued, "what would happen if I spoke to you and you became immediately defensive, sat up rigidly and stared at me angrily. What would I feel and do?"

Both sat silently for a moment.

"You'd probably continue talking, trying to get your point across," Karen said.

"And if I did, what would the result be?"

"Well," Karen continued, "if I didn't want to hear what you were saying, I'd get defensive too and either shut up or argue back."

"Bingo," I said.

"Have you guys been there, done that?"

"Yep," Cole said while Karen nodded.

"Here is the most important thing I'm going to say today. Worth more than the price of admission," I said smiling.

"The process is the problem," I said.

"The process is the problem," I repeated. "Not that Cole has threatened divorce, as hurtful as that feels. Not that Karen has called you names, Cole, as humiliating as that is. The process is the problem leading to arguing and more arguing. If we can change the process, we can change the world."

"I'm not sure I follow," Karen offered.

"I wouldn't expect you to at this point," I said. "These are tools that will take some time to learn."

I continued making my point.

"Have you ever . . .

"Raised your voice louder hoping the other person would listen to you?"

"Continued talking well beyond when the other person had shut down and stopped listening?"

"Debated a point, knowing all the while, you were arguing rather than respectfully discussing a problem?"

"Told the other person their ideas were 'stupid' or 'ridiculous,' or found some other way to put down their ideas?"

"Angrily stormed out of the room, refusing to listen to the other person?"

"Whoa, I think maybe every one of them," Cole admitted sheepishly.

"We do that stuff all the time," Karen said, wiping tears from her eyes.

Most people engage in fruitless arguments. It's not that we're bad people, or that we enjoy fighting. We just want to be heard, understood and validated. We want those around us to really listen to us and take in what we're saying.

"Someone said the highest form of love is to be understood," I said to Karen and Cole. "Do you two love each other?"

"Yes," they both said.

"Do you love each other enough to learn a new skill that will convey beyond a shadow of a doubt that you're sold out for each other?"

Looking at each other, they both nodded.

"Okay," I said, "I'm going to hold you to that. Let's get going and try an experiment."

Neutralizing Arguments

This powerful tool to neutralize arguments is deceptively simple, as are all the tools in our book. While deceptively simple, when used, it has a powerful impact. Simple tool—dynamite impact.

Here it is: *"I love you too much to argue with you. I'm going to stop this discussion until I can calm down and can give you my complete attention."*

That's it! We neutralize arguments by refusing to engage in them. We understand that arguments occur when we're feeling threatened, angry or defensive. We try to "win" arguments as a defense against feeling threatened or insecure. This tool will help us feel more powerful than any assault tactic could ever do, but we must make a new decision: *we refuse to argue.* It's as simple as that.

Of course none of us, as adults, argue. That's what kids do, right? What we do as adults is reason with others so they will understand our point. Unfortunately the unspoken message we send when we try to reason with another adults is, *"I'm sure you looked at all sides of this issue, and somehow you still came up with the stupidest answer. Now I need to straighten you out by telling you how wrong you are or how unfair you are."*

In spite of our our good intentions, or skillful presentation of the facts as we see them, this exercise usually goes south on us. Why is this? Not many of us are good at telling others they are wrong and making friends with them at the same time. Heaven knows, we all try it over and over, and have done so throughout the ages.

What we have just suggested is once you recognize the potential for an argument it is helpful to say, "I love you too much to argue with you." Now this sounds good on the surface and it looks good on paper, but there is a major problem with saying this out loud to another adult if you want to maintain a relationship.

The *Love and Logic* approach teaches parents to say this when they are on the verge of being hooked into an unwinnable argument with their children. And it is highly effective because of the necessary roles the parent plays as both a model and a loving authority figure.

But, ouch! Our roles as equal partners in an adult relationship are different. Saying, "I love you too much to argue," with another adult could put the relationship in jeopardy, or destroy it altogether.

Think It Don't Say It

What's the answer to this dilemma? **Don't say it out loud. Think it to yourself, instead.** This one *thought* may avoid frustration and has been known to save many relationships.

As you read the rest of this chapter remember that each time we write these words, we are suggesting that you *think* this mantra instead of saying it out loud.

A Valuable Alternative

So now, if you find that you just can't let something go and need to say something out loud, we could take a page out of the playbook of one our good friends. I'd swear he had a tatoo of this statement on the inside of his eyelids. Regardless of what another person said, he bought himself valuable time and avoided saying the wrong thing with, "I'm not sure how to react to that. Let me think it over and I'll get back with you."

Neutralizing Arguments

Returning to a discussion with both parties feeling neutral, we fully listen and learn all we can about the other person. We rehearse a critical insight: *I cannot listen to you when I'm feeling defensive or angry, and so I will stop arguing when my anger level becomes too high to listen.*

You control you, and that means you can control when and how you will engage in a discussion. You never have to be lured into a spider web of debate, arguing or wrangling over an issue. You can let the person know that you refuse to engage in fruitless arguments.

"I love/like you too much to argue with you. I'm going to stop arguing until I calm down and can give you my complete attention."

Can you see the gift in this tool?

- When I refuse to argue, calming myself down, I am better able to *listen* to what you have to say.
- When I refuse to argue, calming myself down, I am better able to *learn* the message you want to give me.
- When I refuse to argue, calming myself down, I am better able to *validate* your point of view, even if I don't agree with it.
- When I refuse to argue, calming myself down, I'm better able to *understand* where you're coming from.

- When I refuse to argue with you, calming myself down, I am better able to *be influenced by your message, allowing it to impact and perhaps even change me.*

Can you feel the power of this tool? By refusing to argue, mastering the art of being non-defensive, I will show my respect for you by really listening.

There is something quite enchanting that happens when others feel listened to. When angry people feel understood and validated, they calm down. When hurt and frustrated people feel cared about and their message is making an impact, they feel loved.

Refusing to argue, and more important, focusing on creating an inner space where you can attend to the people in your life, will build a bridge in your relationships, allowing positive feelings to flow back and forth freely.

Anatomy of an Argument

Arguing seems to be everywhere, but we're about to put an end to it in your life. The beauty of neutralizing arguments is we end petty arguments, creating a path to understanding each other. Few people want to argue. Arguing is draining, discouraging and causes damaging dissension in a relationship. If you've been arguing with your friends, chances are you feel detached from them, perhaps to the point of wondering if the relationship is worth saving.

If arguing is so destructive, and it is, why do we do it?

We argue because we're trying, quite ineffectively, to obtain the five things listed above. Let's examine them more closely.

One, *we want to be heard.* We will go to nearly any extreme to be heard. We'll shout, bully, browbeat, even call names if we think we will get someone to hear us.

Of course these tactics don't work, and in fact, cause even greater distance. But, wanting to be listened to, we will use these old tactics, trying to force our mate to hear us.

Let's find a new way.

Second, *we want others to learn about us*. We want people to care about what we're thinking, feeling and what we want. We're desperate for someone to care enough to sit and listen to the ache in our hearts, and we'll stop at nothing to get that to happen. Again, destructive tactics only serve to worsen the situation.

Let's find a new way.

Third, *we want others to understand us*. In our desperate effort to be understood, we often use words, words and more words, failing to recognize others have tuned us out by our overload of words.

When words fail, we resort to emotion. And more emotion. We raise our voices, become more passionate about what is bothering us, all in the effort to be understood. Again, we fail to fully appreciate that these tactics don't work.

Let's find a new way.

Fourth, *we want our message to be validated*. We want our friends not only to listen to us, learning about us in the process, but also understand and validate our message. We desperately want others to look at us and say, "You have a right to feel what you're feeling."

Let's find a new way.

Finally, *we want others to be influenced by our message*. It does little good if we share our thoughts, feelings and needs to only have them ignored and disregarded. If we've asked for something very important, and then feel dismissed, we're likely to be angrier and more hurt than when we began.

Let's find a new way.

We don't simply want these five qualities in our relationships—we need them. They are like air and water to a relationship. Without them we fight, struggle and argue to get them. They are mandatory to healthy relationships.

The New Way

What if we decided to offer these five gifts freely, without restraint to the people in our lives? What if we didn't have to fight for them? Would you be interested in relationships where these five gifts were given freely, with the understanding that you *refuse to argue and will calm yourself down so you can fully attend to the people in your life?*

As hard as this principle appears, when I focus on refusing to argue, I'm able to be fully present to my family, friends and associates, faults and all. I'm able to remain calm and not get hooked into fruitless arguments.

When I remain calm, reminding myself of my intent not to argue, I'm able to interact effectively with store clerks, (as well as friends and family), whether they are respectful to me or not. I set my own agenda aside in favor of truly listening. Calmed and centered—repeated as necessary!—my mood and ability to interact effectively are not dependent on others.

Remember the endless bickering of Karen and Cole, who battled each other in a fruitless effort to be heard? They are beginning to practice this new tool with amazing results. Their marriage is strengthening as they learn to truly listen to each other and refuse to engage in arguing. They are learning how to set aside their desire to defend, become angry or make a point. They want to neutralize their arguments.

When trying to sell people on this new way of interacting, we're often met with, "What about them? What if other people don't play fair? What if they want to hook us into arguing with them?"

These are all reasonable questions, all with the same answer. The New Way calls for us letting go of our fear of being criticized. The New Way involves trusting the process—that if we don't engage in fruitless arguing, refusing to get 'hooked,' we trust others to take care of us. Instead of retaliating, we decide to set the tone for conversations. These are new, incredibly powerful choices for you.

We've become so excited about the truth that one person can set the climate for a relationship. Since emotions are contagious, we embrace the power we have to influence others. We can choose to slide into needless arguing, or we can smile, speak a soft word, and voice our desire to get along.

Can you see the opportunity in the New Way? Here is your opportunity to give to yourself and your friends an incredible gift—*the gift of refusing to argue*, taking time to calm yourself, truly listening and understanding others.

You can start today by:

- offering to listen to others whenever they have something to say;
- offering to set your inner "chatter" of defensiveness aside so you attend to others;
- offering to learn more about others and what is important to them;
- offering to fully understand others and the importance of their message;
- offering to validate another's points of view and their right to think the way they think, even if you disagree with it;
- offering to be influenced by another's message.

Giving these gifts to yourself and others will have a profound impact on your life. Be prepared for your life to blossom. Be prepared for your friends to begin relating with you in deeper ways than you imagined possible. Prepare for powerful and healthy change.

Cell Phone Store

I was fully anticipating another fruitless argument the day I went to the cell phone store. With a history of troubling experiences with this cell phone store, I walked into the store with more than an ounce of trepidation.

I had done the unthinkable, dropping my cell phone in the hot tub, and along with it, countless contacts, emails, phone numbers and appointment dates.

Panicked, annoyed and expecting the fight of my life, I tiptoed into the store. I was amped up and ready for an impending challenge. Putting my name on the list, I waited for my turn. I dreaded this moment, fearing a power struggle.

Calling my number, I headed for the counter. The Customer Service Representative asked, "What can I do for you?"

Feeling irritated and expecting an argument, I said, "I always dread coming in here because I have to wait. If my phone wasn't so important to me, believe me, I wouldn't be in here."

Armed with the tool of *neutralizing arguments*, he offered, "Boy, I hear you. Our phones have become our lifeline. I want to make this experience work for you. What can I do for you today?"

I began to calm down and let out a huge sigh. Maybe this wasn't going to be an argument. My defenses were lowered and I instantly felt connected to this person. I sensed that he really wanted to help me. Feeling validated, I was defused and ready to talk about what needed to happen to solve my problems.

The next several minutes were not only calm and easy, but extremely relieving. I developed a connection with the Customer Service Representative who worked with me to retrieve my emails, phone numbers and contacts. He helped me obtain a new phone and reestablish my cell phone needs.

While this experience was obviously made easier by the cell phone clerk, you too can adopt this strategy in every walk of life. You too can decide to refuse to argue in every situation—you carry with you this powerful tool and resolve not to argue. You can defuse potentially conflicting situations, creating a powerful relationship with everyone in your world. That kind of power is in your hands.

Jim shared the following story with me:

"I watched with great interest, amazement, and gratitude, this skill (neutralizing arguments) being used by a United Airlines ticket agent one day. Attempting to catch an earlier flight, I raced into the Salt Lake airport with just a few minutes to spare. Luckily, there was only one person in line in front of me.

Unfortunately, she was what you might call a high maintenance woman, draped in furs and jewels. She was demanding the airlines trade a super saver, non-refundable ticket for a regular ticket on a different flight.

Her body language screeched power, influence, and impatience. You could tell she was used to getting her way. Turning to me, she said in a rather loud voice, "If I don't get my way on this, I'm really going to get mad!"

"I'm afraid this is going to cost you an extra $180.00," the agent said.

"But you don't understand," she yelled. "I have a good reason for needing to change this ticket."

In a calm voice, the ticket agent responded, "I'm sure that's true, ma'am, and the cost will be $180.00."

"This is ridiculous. My husband expects me to be home on this flight, not the other one."

"I'm sure that's true, and I have to charge the additional fee."

*"Well, this is stupid. My husband flies this airline every week, and if I don't get this without the charge, we'll **never** fly United again!"*

"I'm sure that's true, and how do you want to handle the $180.00?"

"Oh, will you take a credit card?"

She slammed the credit card on the counter with a huge sigh. The exchange was completed quickly and I still had time to change my ticket and be on my way to my plane on time. Had the agent chosen to argue, I would have missed my opportunity to get home early."

Why did this technique work so well for the agent? It was because he validated each of her responses while sticking to one and only one statement, "I'm sure that's true, and . . ." Not only is it important to use a neutralizing argument statement, is also important to play "broken record" with the statement. If he had used a different statement each time, he would have provided something different for her to argue with each time. If that had happened, Jim would've missed his plane.

"By the way," Jim said as he finished sharing this story, "I took a couple of minutes to congratulate the agent on his skill. My guess is that an agent with this level of skill has far less stress than those who don't."

Helping Your Friends Give to You

Making this decision makes you a hero, much like the Customer Service Representative in the cell phone store and the United ticket agent. By refusing to argue, and seeking ways of connecting to others, you offer the most incredible gift imaginable. You are the hero by refusing to argue with anyone in your world.

In another way, you are assisting your friends, family and work world in offering you a priceless gift. You're not going to walk away from these interactions empty-handed. When you make the decision to refuse to argue, the argument ends. It takes two to tango, so if you're not dancing, the dance is over. However, there are some things you can do to enhance the possibility that your friends will buy into giving these gifts on a regular basis.

It is critical that your friends understand your intention—that you want to fully attend to them. They must understand you want to learn more about them, meeting their legitimate needs. They must also understand you cannot do that when you are too angry, defensive, or caught in a power struggle. So, you need their help. What can you ask for?

Ask them to make this agreement with you: *We refuse to argue with one another. We like each other too much to argue with one another. We're going to stop this discussion until we can calm down, giving each other our complete attention. We agree to seek solutions that benefit each other."*

Making this decision, and agreement, will transform any relationship. Decide that bickering, debating, browbeating and other hostile forms of coercion are strictly off limits. Join in the endeavor to neutralize arguments, knowing that the degree to which you are successful is the same degree to which you'll be able to offer them the five powerful gifts.

Making this offer to your friends and family is not only a way to stabilize any relationship, but will increase the level of understanding and connection. I can't imagine your family and friends will turn their nose up at this incredible opportunity. Seek their assistance with these goals. See if they're willing to try out these new behaviors and see what happens.

Four Basic Principals of Love and Logic Revisited

As I consider my family gathering, the clerk at the department store, working with Karen and Cole and talking to the cell phone representative, I'm reminded of the importance of the four basic principals of *Love and Logic*, and how they apply to relationships. These four powerful principles need to be a central part of every relationship.

Let's review these basic principles:

- *We always maintain the dignity of individuals:* Everyone desires to be treated with dignity. There is never a need to shame or disrespect another person.
- *We share control:* We share control over how we're going to solve problems. We understand you control your feelings and actions, I control my feelings and actions, and we control our relationship.
- *We share the thinking:* It is up to us to think about our problems. We negotiate with one another over the direction of our relationship.
- *We follow an empathy/consequence formula:* We work together to develop healthy boundaries, and understand empathy is the glue that holds us together. We feel sorry when we violate another's boundaries, and understand we'll need to make amends to another if we harm them.

The next time I'm with a disrespectful store clerk, I will choose to refuse to engage in an argument. When with my family, I'll celebrate their unique personalities while setting boundaries on how they interact with me. I'll neutralize arguments largely by refusing to engage in them.

Consider how you might use these principles in your daily life. How might you use these principles in your marriage, workplace friendships, or even relationship with your boss? Armed with these principles, refusing to engage in arguments and practicing the empathy/consequence formula, one person can change a relationship—and that's pretty powerful stuff!

A Passion for Peace

"I just want peace."

This is a common refrain spoken by many people. Wanting peace, and getting it, however, are two very different things.

What if you could live peacefully 99 percent of the time? Would you like that? Are you open to the possibility that you can live in peace and spend your time cultivating a relationship rather than protecting your individual turf? It's very possible.

The path to peace requires not only *neutralizing arguments*, but one more powerful tool. I am giving it to you for free. It's a bonus.

Cooperation. (It's taught on Sesame Street.)

Cooperation means that you let go of your fighting for your individual rights, considering the larger picture. The larger picture pertains to us/we. Rather than being two people living in the same house, you are a couple sharing your hearts, lives, dreams and goals. Rather than working for a corporation, you're part of a team of people with similar goals. Rather than friends with differing needs, you value common goals and needs. But, you must have *cooperation* to obtain these goals.

To reach this place called cooperation you must be willing to give up rigid positions, staked-out points of view and dogmatic ideas. You must let go of any need to be *right*.

This is hard to do if you have rigid perceptions of family, with whom you've been interacting in a certain way for years. You will need a great deal of self-awareness and self-control to change habitual ways of interacting.

Department stores and cell phone stores are where we spend much of our lives, and are often places of tension. Here, too, are places to practice *neutralizing arguments*. Any place where two people share differing points of view are places for us to latch onto *Love and Logic* tools.

My family had much to learn about *neutralizing arguments* and cooperation. Karen and Cole had much to learn, but they were willing to try out some new ways of behaving. I learned much from the cell phone representative. We're all learning the importance of refusing to argue, understanding we alone are responsible for managing our defensiveness. It is up to each of us to completely listen to the other, ending our petty bickering.

As much as it is tempting to only look out for ourselves, if we really want to *neutralize arguments* and live peacefully, we must be as concerned about another's well-being as our own. This can be really tough, especially if we're bothered by them. But, think about it: we need the people in our lives to be happy, and if we can be instrumental in bringing happiness into their lives—and we can!—why not do it?

So, are you ready to create happiness around you? Are you ready to take a special interest in how your friends are doing? Can you show empathy and compassion for your boss, though you may not like all of his/her actions and policies? Will you work hard to understand your mate? If so, get ready for a big change in your life.

Run This Experiment

Consider your world. Where do you find yourself experiencing the most tension? Is it at work, where you struggle to get along with your work mates? Is it with your boss, finding him/her to be demanding and challenging? Perhaps it is in your marriage or friendships, where you seem to create and experience conflict at every turn.

It doesn't really matter where you have the most trouble—you can control your situation by changing your approach. I want you to try this experiment:

In addition to *refusing to argue*, practice applying these principles to every interaction and notice the results:

- listen to others whenever they have something to say;
- learn more about others and what is important to them;
- fully understand others and the importance of their message;
- validate another's point of view and their right to think the way they think, even if you disagree with it;
- be influenced by another's message.

After reading this, you might think that we are saying to give in and let other people walk all over you. **Not true.** Think back to the United ticket agent. Did he give up and give in? No, not at all. He got his way and he did it the easy, stress free way.

Learning to *neutralize arguments* is the first powerful tool in our book. It is the foundation to the other tools you will learn in this book.

2

Delaying Consequences

"You need an infinite stretch of time ahead of you to start to think, infinite energy to make the smallest decision."

—JEAN BAUDRILLAR

Fences make great neighbors, unless your neighbor erects fences without checking in with you first.

Janice had sharp words with her neighbor, Jack, who took it upon himself to start putting up a fence without talking to Janice and Gary. Jack was out measuring for his fence when she noticed him.

"What'cha doing, Jack?" Janice shouted from our deck.

"I'm building a fence," he replied nonchalantly.

"Hey, maybe we need to talk about this," she said as she hurried over to where he was working.

After getting to where he was working, she continued talking.

"Are you sure you know where the boundary lines are?" she asked.

"Well," he said, "I think I know."

"Do you know what the legal setbacks are?" she asked.

"No, I don't," he said.

"Well, shouldn't you have talked this over with Gary and me?"

"No," he said. "I don't think this has anything to do with you and Gary. We have a right to put up a fence on our property."

With that Janice came into the house extremely agitated and called Gary at work.

"I only answer for my wife," He said, glancing at his client. "What's up?"

Janice ranted and raved for a few moments as he tried to calm her down. Boy, was she reeling from her interaction with the neighbor.

"What are we going to do?" she said.

"I'm not sure," he told her. "That's a lot of stuff, Janice. I have to think about it."

"But, he's building the fence right now and I need to know what to do," she said, still quite angry.

"I understand you're feeling anxious about this," he assured her, "but I'm not sure what we should say. I think our first task is to calm down, sit back and ponder the situation."

"I can't sit back and ponder anything," she said with obvious frustration. "We need to know what to do now!"

"No we don't," he said matter-of-factly. "Sometimes the best thing to do is *nothing*. When we speak out of our frustration and anger, generally nothing good comes from it. Sometimes the best thing we can do is settle down, reflect and then offer a more considered opinion and course of action. We can decide what the reasonable consequences for his actions are later."

"Okay," she said slowly. "I guess I understand that. So, can you and I brainstorm possible courses of action?"

"Sure," he said. "But again, I think we should be prepared to do nothing. We may or may not come up with something appropriate. The first thing to do is *nothing*, giving us time to consider the situation and talk to him after I get off work. This situation calls for delaying consequences, not impulsive reaction."

"I guess that makes sense," she said. "So, delay any heavy conversations?"

"That's right. Why don't you go call or visit a friend, take care of yourself. If you call me later this afternoon, we can brainstorm solutions and consequences then."

Keep the Reaction to Yourself But Delay Your Actions

What he asked Janice to do was completely against what feels normal. In any crisis we want to act, take charge, make something happen. We want to feel like we're in control, but usually our efforts are random and only make matters worse.

What if you could give yourself permission to step back from a problem, deciding not to react, but to consider a situation before responding? Would you feel more in control? What if you made a point of not reacting, but always prepared the time, place and circumstances for any serious conversation?

Of course this goes against our nature. We want quick solutions, quick decisions, quick actions. We want to dive in, head first, no matter how shallow the water is or how great the risk of breaking our necks. We're impulsive, reactive, emotion-driven people. But, this never works in the arena of relating. Just as surely as this kind of reactivity creates havoc in child-discipline, it also creates horrific problems in the arena of relating as well.

Consider the consequences of reactivity:

- We make impulsive decisions
- We make emotion-driven decisions
- We often are harsh, punitive and critical
- We often regret what we've said or done
- We rarely get what we want

Now, let's remind ourselves of the principles from the pioneers of the *Love and Logic* Institute that drive our behavior. With this wisdom clearly in place, we use consequences in such a way as to:

- Maintain the dignity of individuals
- Share control
- Share the thinking
- Use consequences *with empathy*

Using consequences effectively, everyone knows exactly where they stand. Your friends and family know clearly what you want, what you'll tolerate and what you won't. Likewise, you know where they stand, what they will tolerate and what they won't. Consequences are the boundaries that increase the likelihood that those things will happen, creating a wonderful and dynamic relationship.

A couple of weeks before the fence episode, Christie and I were returning from a trip to Mexico. I asked her to run grab us a snack for the flight, which she kindly did. However, when they started boarding the flight she was nowhere to be found. Tired, irritable and ready to be home, I panicked.

As people began to board the plane, my panic led to irritation and quickly escalated to anger. Before long Christie came, loaded with snacks, but unprepared for my anger. I immediately, *reactively*, scolded her and gave her the silent treatment for the next hour. She then decided not to talk to me, since I had been so irritable. I was surprised by her distance, and then became upset at her for not talking to me. Talk about the "snowball effect."

"David," she said firmly, seated next to me at 36,000 feet, "if you're going to scold me and treat me badly, I'm going to read my book. Maybe we can carry on this discussion at a better time."

Holy cow! She meant business.

"Fine," I said, acting all tough and macho, but still flooded with emotion.

After a few minutes, however, this was not fine. I didn't like the distance between us. I had to decide if I was going to continue and pout, or apologize. I had to reflect on my actions and what I wanted to say to her. Calmed down and having considered the situation, I chose to talk to her in a respectful manner.

Over the next several minutes we talked the situation over—rationally. Having taken time to calm down and reflect, I could see the situation much more rationally. I was no longer a babbling idiot, but was able, *through delaying consequences*, to decide how I wanted to act—not react.

Now, this scenario is probably not only familiar to you, but you might be wondering why I was surprised at her reaction. Every action, remember, leads to a reaction. Christie decided that if I was going to treat her badly, she was going to have nothing to do with me. Not rocket science here. Every action usually leads to a consequence of some kind, and in this chapter we want to learn to manage those consequences effectively.

While I'm a rather slow learner, I'm figuring out that if I treat her badly, she will either treat me just as badly—if she's not in her best space—or she'll make it clear that she won't be treated that way. She's come to master the art of using consequences effectively, and you can too!

Chaos

Reactivity creates one thing—chaos! I have never seen anything good come from an impulsive reaction. People who fail to use the delayed consequence technique often find themselves knee-deep in the mire of conflict.

Now what about the neighbor who was building the fence without consulting the bordering neighbors? Did Christie have a right to react? Doesn't she have a right to "lay down the law," and pin his ears to the wall?

Hopefully you can see such a reaction will lead to only one thing—more chaos and bad feelings. You can see that if she *reacts without delaying consequences*, this relationship might spiral out of control. Remember, delaying consequences doesn't mean having no reaction—only taking the time to choose how you will respond, and then to make responsible choices.

Chaotic. This is the one word that describes the majority of relationships, and is primarily the result of poor boundaries and the absence of consequences.

Yes, without consequences there is chaos, and none of us can live effectively without some sense of order and predictability in our lives.

When you look closely at most relationships, you wonder about their Rules of Engagement. In other words, what are the principles governing the way they talk to each other? How do they make amends for mistakes? Are there remedies they set into motion to make their relationship run smoother?

Many people, and perhaps you are one of them, seem to bounce from one altercation to another. They move from one challenging interaction to another, often escalating, and ending in a blowout. Things settle down until the next escalation occurs. It's no wonder we are exhausted.

No one is guiding the ship, and as a result, there are far too many bumps and bruises along the way from the icebergs they hit.

If the captain of the Titanic had heeded the warnings given to him repeatedly, thousands of lives would have been saved and the Titanic would still be making Trans-Atlantic cruises. But, he didn't and the consequences were horrific.

Managing Consequences

So, if we're not going to react, what are we supposed to do? The answer is quite simple. It is best to learn to manage your reaction and then to delay and manage consequences. Don't worry, you can do this!

Every action leads to a reaction or consequence. As we move through this book, you'll become more effective at watching your actions and the consequent reactions of your mate. You'll start to notice patterns, seeing how some actions are effective, while others are absolutely disastrous. The disastrous ones are particularly instructive because they scream at us: YIKES! DON'T EVEN THINK ABOUT DOING THAT AGAIN.

I really hate those, but must admit those mistakes teach me powerful lessons. When Christie chose not to talk to me on the plane, I had several hours of silence to remind me that she demanded being treated with respect.

Her reaction didn't surprise me. Why would she tolerate my actions? Any self-respecting person is going to insist on being treated
with respect. While we may not always follow through on consequences—and that is the focus of this chapter—we all feel the
desire to put up boundaries to behavior that makes us feel bad.

I'm working with a couple, Sam and Kathy, who have been
married for seven years. Sam, a serious-minded businessman with
a wry sense of humor, is particularly frustrated with Kathy, a witty
but scattered woman. He is repeatedly troubled about her spending, which she admits has always been out of control. She consistently overdraws her checking account, paying late fees. They fight
about money continuously and have come to me for counsel.

Within a few minutes of our first session it was clear to me that
not only do they disagree on how to spend money, but the way
they fight is destructive and disrespectful, violating the *Love and
Logic* principles.

I began our work by teaching them the four principles of *Love
and Logic*, showing them how we could weave these principles into
our work. We had to find a solution where neither felt disrespect-
ed, where both shared control, where we problem-solved together
and finally, and where there would be consequences for violated
agreements.

Both were enthusiastic about the first three, but Kathy squirmed
when we talked about consequences.

"This feels like I'm being treated like a child," Kathy protested.

"I don't understand," I said. "What don't you like about this
process? You will participate in the agreement, never be disrespect-
ed, but there will be consequences for both of you if you fail to live
by those agreements."

"Hmm," Kathy said, "I guess if we both live by our agreements,
it seems fair."

"Of course," I said, matter-of-factly, "we all have to live with agreements and the consequences of failing to live by those agreements."

We set out to find a solution to their money problems. We me-
thodically reviewed their finances and discussed how each wanted

to spend and save their money. They made agreements and set consequences for any violation of their agreement. They agreed, however, never to react, but to experiment with the tool of delaying consequences (reactions) whenever they were too emotional or in doubt about a situation.

In this particular case, Kathy and Sam agreed that if Kathy overdrew their checking account, she would have to work overtime at her job to pay the extra fees. Within a few months, and one time of having to work overtime to pay her overdraft fines, she was cured.

Notice the process. Both sat down and talked in a respectful way to discuss their problem. Both managed their emotions and were non-reactive. Both were involved in finding a solution. Both agreed upon the solution. Powerful stuff!

What are Consequences?

If you're like me, you probably think consequences are only for kids. We left them back in the folder titled, *Disciplinary Actions For Our Kids*. Well, guess what? I want you to dig out that folder and consider the possibility of trying out some of those strategies in your adult relationships. Yes, the same tools we used on our children can be effective in our adult relationships.

But, isn't using *consequences* with adults childish? Not at all. With adults we allow consequences to fall on their own rather than imposing them. In relationships, consequences fall into place when the other person does not rescue you from your actions. In fact, as you saw from my recent experience with Christie, she used consequences quite effectively with me.

Consider the issue of *consequences* as it pertains to the real world, which is what we always want to model our actions against. Just as we want to teach our children to learn to navigate through the real world effectively, we want to teach others around us how to navigate through the world of relationships effectively. Consider these everyday examples of consequences:

- You choose to show up for work late consistently: *pink slip!*
- You choose to drive over the speed limit: *yellow slip!*
- You choose to stay in a parking spot longer than your allotted time: *green slip!*
- You choose to not follow building code regulations: *orange slip!*
- And what do we call each of these situations? *A slip up!!*

The point is, there are consequences to our actions in the real world, and these consequences teach us lessons. We learn not to show up for work late, not to drive over the speed limit, not to park too long on the street, not to disregard building codes, and last, not to scold our wives.

Law and Order

While none of us enjoys being on the receiving end of these *slips*, at some level we appreciate them because they create law and order. For as much as we like doing our own thing, doing our own thing creates chaos, and that's not always healthy for our relationship.

Imagine a world where there was no predictability, no law and order, and only chaos. Imagine if there were no rules, no principles or no guidelines. What would happen if I told my boss I would show up for work when I felt like it, and would get the job done at my own pace? What would happen if I drove any speed I liked, in any direction I liked, any time I liked?

Now transfer this attitude to our relationships. What happens if I act any way I want to my friends? What happens if I say what I want to say, do what I want to do and go where I want to go?

The answer is simple: *chaos!*

We must have order in our world, and that order comes in the form of *consequences*—sometimes delayed, sometimes immediate, always considered. We must become effective at learning to use consequences to our benefit and to the benefit of the relationship. Consequences bring predictability, which leads to trust and security. These are critical ingredients to any relationship.

Choosing the Consequence

I suspect your mind is swirling with different scenarios that create havoc in your relationships. That's good! I want you to think about possibilities, where these principles and strategies could bring harmony back to your relationships.

What kind of consequences do you use with a grown man or woman? Again, our minds are stuck in thinking consequences only belong in the world of discipline with children. This is not true. We use consequences every day with our friends and loved ones— *but we use them inconsistently, creating chaos.*

We must become much more effective in choosing which consequences are effective in the world of adults. Obviously, we cannot ground our bosses or send them to their rooms. We can't take away their television privileges. So what can we do? This is an incredibly important question and one that we'll answer later in this book. For now, however, it is enough to simply understand that we must become comfortable with the issue of consequences for irresponsible behavior or violated agreements.

How do we choose consequences? This can be a bit tricky, but once you get the hang of it, it comes easier. The primary principle to follow is that consequences must be agreed upon by both parties, and should be "natural" if possible. Here are a few examples:

- Your roommate refuses to wipe his feet at the door: *He agrees to clean the carpets.*
- Your husband refuses to come home on time for dinner: *He agrees to eat a cold dinner or fix his own meal.*
- Your officemate refuses not to use swear words when angry: *She agrees to participate in an eight hour Anger Management workshop.*

I'm sure you get the idea. Agreed upon problem. Agreed upon solution, always using natural consequences.

Delaying Consequences or Actions

One of the most important principles when it comes to consequences is giving yourself permission to delay them. If there's a consequence worth delivering, it's worth delaying.

I suppose you're scratching your head at those words. After all, like I've said, we're used to reacting—now! We're used to making idle threats, over-reacting and having angry outbursts. But, in the last chapter you learned the value and power of neutralizing arguments, and now we want to build on this incredible tool. In addition to using consequences, we also want to learn the power of delaying consequences.

What if you gave yourself permission to never react? Yes, you read correctly. Never react. What if you could trust yourself to never react because you knew you needed time to think before discussing the situation, delaying consequences? Would you be interested? Of course you would.

I remember when I was a kid, I built a rocket ship. Not one that was too fancy, mind you, but one that was capable of flying high enough to land on our roof. Propelled by pressurized water, I would pump up the rocket, push the release button and excitedly watch my personal spacecraft soar into the heavens.

However, before going too far with my personal space mission, I had to secure the launch pad. I cleared an area for the rocket. I moved my buddies out of the way, preparing to scramble for safety as well. I followed the instructions explicitly so nothing too disastrous happened. I took time in the preparatory phase so the launch was as exciting as possible.

Delaying consequences is a bit like preparing the launch pad. It involves creating a safe place so meaningful conversation can take place. It requires creating an easy and open heart so you can say what you have to say calmly, with conviction. It means anticipating the worst scenario so you'll know ahead of time how you're going to react—er, I mean act.

Back to the Neighbor's Fence Dilemma

Janice and Gary decided to take some time to calm down. They thought about the consequences Jack might face if he built the fence in the wrong place. "I guess he'd have to deal with the city and pay for a surveyor. The consequences will fall on their own," said Janice. "There is no need for us to ruin our relationship over his lack of planning."

The next day Janice knocked on Jack's door saying, "Jack, I got pretty upset when I saw the fence, but after thinking about it I know you have every right to build it. Our friendship is too important to ruin over a fence."

"To tell the truth, Janice, I didn't want to have to build the stupid thing in the first place. But I guess you don't know that my mom died and promised her I would take care of her big dog. I didn't want him to be a problem for you, so that's why I'm doing it."

"Wow, I understand, Jack. I guess neither one of us wants a fence back there, but are you sure you're not putting it in the wrong place? If we go to sell some day, I'm sure the buyer will want proof that it's not over our line."

As Janice walked away she thought, "Geez, his mom died and I almost made a jerk out of myself over the fence. It's a good thing I delayed on this."

The Land of Idle Threats

Reactivity leads to saying things we don't mean, making threats we never fully intend to keep. Permission to delay consequences gives us invaluable time to settle down and fully consider any given problem.

We live in The Land of Idle Threats. How many times have you used, or heard the following:

"If you ever do that again, I'll . . ."
"You can't treat me that way."
"This is intolerable."

What invariably happens next? *We tolerate it! We don't follow through with any consequences. We complain, argue, debate, threaten.*

And then what happens? *We go on with life.*

Now, what I hope jumps out at you is that when we go on with life, when our threats fall to the ground like crumbs from last night's dinner, our words become powerless. Our threats become just another glomp of meaningless words. We lose our power and our credibility.

If you're comparing these behaviors to the parent who threatens a kid, *and then does nothing,* you're right. Big words, little action. Loud bark, little bite. We hear this person roar, but then watch him/her leave the room squealing.

Another couple I worked with had been arguing and bickering for years. They had grown accustomed to their arguing, and only shrugged when the other was displeased.

The wife, Katie, decided it was time to try something new, and made an appointment with me. Her husband, Jack, refused the invitation to join her for the session.

"What brings you here?" I asked Katie.

"My husband and I have been married thirteen years, and most of them have been unpleasant," she said, her voice sounding vacant and as collapsed as her slumped posture in the chair. "We argue and fight and the intimacy between us gets less all the time."

"By the way," I said, "where is your husband? Why isn't he here with you?"

"Probably the same answer as to why we're still bickering after all these years. He sees no real reason for change, so here I am."

"Hmm. Tell me again how you encouraged him to be here," I said.

"Well," she said softly, with a hint of irritation in her voice, "I asked him to come and he said 'no.'"

"Anything else?" I asked quizzically.

"No. I don't know what else to do."

"I suggest we experiment with a few things," I said. "Now, none of these experiments are guaranteed to work, but if you're game, we'll try a few different things. We'll always treat him with respect, but we need to add a few consequences for his choice not to work on a dysfunctional marriage. Don't you agree?"

"Yes," Katie said quickly. "But again, I don't know what to do."

"We'll get that figured out. But for now, we'll delay consequences until we figure it out."

With that we set out to accurately size up the problem and apply the principle of natural consequences. Katie worked hard to discern what might be a natural consequence and develop the courage to follow through. Consistency along with consequences, turned out to be a powerful combination.

Over the next few weeks Katie discovered ways to end her part in their arguments. She refused to "bite" on his provocations. She also made it clear that if Jack was unwilling to come to counseling, she would no longer act as if nothing were wrong. She would be cordial, but nothing more. She calmly laid out her reasoning, refusing to engage in arguing about counseling. She didn't threaten to leave him, but suggested there might be more serious consequences if he was not willing to work on their relationship together.

Run This Experiment

It's time for you to consider your relationships. How do you handle problems? Are you reactive, making idle threats? Are you ready to delay consequences, and then willing to consider the best consequences for your circumstances? As you reflect on your problems, with a clear, calm mind, you're certain to come up with some reasonable courses of action.

Here's where I'd like you to begin:

Sit down with someone close to you and come up with a problem you've been unable to solve. Make something up if you have to. It's an experiment. Decide you're going to talk calmly, with the idea that whatever you agree upon *is just an experiment—it's okay to fail. You'll just try something new.*

Now that you've agreed upon a problem, see if you can find a solution *with boundaries and consequences.* Make the consequences something you both can live with. Also agree to find an opportunity to delay consequences when facing a new problem. See how it works.

You're well on your way to changing how you and your mate deal with problems. By embracing the *Love and Logic* principles, adding tools such as *neutralizing arguments and delaying consequences*, you're going to notice some powerful changes. In the next chapter we'll see how *the power of empathy* will add even more to your set of skills and momentum.

3

Unleashing the Power of Empathy

*"For it was not into my ear you whispered, but into my heart.
It was not my lips you kissed, but my soul."*

—JUDY GARLAND

Are you getting excited about the power of *Love and Logic* tools?
Although initially created for use with kids, you can see they are
equally powerful with adults. You can never have enough tools to
build strong relationships. Right?

As with children, you can use these tools in your adult relationships one at a time, or in combination. Don't forget, if one doesn't
work, try another.

At this stage of the game you're starting to see how these tools all
fit together. First you learned about the power of *neutralizing arguments*, then practicing the art of *delaying consequences*, and now we
want to give you another potent tool for your toolbox: *unleashing the
power of empathy*.

We attach empathy to consequences with children. When they
fail to follow our family guidelines, they learn best when we show
them we care, even as we remind them of agreed upon consequences.

Empathy tells them we understand how disappointing it will be not to be with their friends that evening because of their irresponsibility, or that plans for playing outdoors are over because of their failure to do their chores.

This same pattern—using empathy with consequences—applies to adults as well. The application for this tool is incredible. I found it amazingly useful when raising my boys, and now apply it to my marriage, friendships, family and workmates. I think you're going to be surprised at how effective it is.

Being inspired, I decided to give these *Love and Logic* tools a test run with a woman I saw recently in a counseling situation. An energetic forty-five-year-old mother of three, Lynne came to her latest counseling situation feeling exasperated about her husband, Don.

"What's the problem?" I asked her.

Clearly frustrated, Lynne launched into a tirade about how irresponsible her husband had been with their family finances.

"He spends more than we have," Lynne said forcefully. "He goes online and makes purchases we don't need. When I catch him buying things, he acts sorry for the moment, and then does it again later a day or two later. No matter how many lectures I give him, it does no good. I'm furious."

I could see the tension written on Lynne's face. The more she shared, the more I was reminded of situations like this between parents and children, where parents become *Helicopter Parents* in an effort to *make* their children become responsible. Of course this never works, and Lynne's efforts at forcing her husband be become more responsible were backfiring.

"What in the world am I doing wrong?" she asked increduloulsy. "I shouldn't have to parent my husband to stop overspending. I'm not his mother!"

"You know, Lynne," I said. "I hear your incredible frustration. I can feel your anger at catching Don being irresponsible. You're absolutely right, by the way. You shouldn't have to parent him and we're going to find a way out of this mess."

Lynne let out a huge sigh, obviously appreciating the empathy I expressed for her dilemna.

"I'd love that. Anything. Tell me anything to get out of this mess. I know Don hates me nagging at him as much as I hate nagging him."

"Well," I said, "you've just said something very important. He probably does hate you nagging him. We've got to engage him in this problem and seek a solution he can live with. We have to empathize with his feelings and encourage him to listen to yours."

"But I don't want to sympathize with him," she said angrily. "I'm angry at him."

"I didn't say *sympathize* Lynne. I said *empathize*, and there's a big difference between them."

"Like what?" she asked.

"Sympathy is feeling sorry for him," I explained, "while empathy means we understand what it's like to walk in his shoes."

"Yeah, I can imagine being in his shoes is no fun right now," she said. "I know he has his side of the story to tell."

"Do you think he would come in and tell his side of the story?"

"Oh, absolutely," she said. "He'll do anything to get me off his back."

"Fantastic!" I said excitedly. "All systems 'go!' "

I was all geared up not only to show them the power of empathy, but the other tools you've learned so far in this book too. This could be fun!

I met the following week with both Don and Lynne. The results were amazing. Not surprisingly, Don resented being treated like a child. He didn't like his wife rifling through his pockets looking for receipts, or scolding him like a child for spending money he felt was justified.

At each stage of telling his story, I encouraged his wife to pay close attention to his feelings and empathize with them. While this took effort, she was able to do it, to his satisfaction.

On the other hand, we also worked with Don, helping him feel the affect his behavior had on his wife. He hadn't fully appreciated how much his spending had impacted her. The energy he previously spent defending himself was now spent empathizing with her, influencing him to seek a reasonable solution to their problem.

Eureka! I felt like I had discovered gold. Listening to each other, really hearing what each other was saying, encouraged change. Helping them empathize with each other created an opening for a new way of interacting. This led to both talking to each other in an adult to adult manner, complete with healthy expectations and boundaries. We had unleashed the power of empathy in their relationship.

"We rarely feel like offering understanding when our bucket is dry," I explained to both of them. "When we feel understood by the other, we naturally feel like cooperating. It's a powerful concept. Criticism doesn't work—empathy does!"

Lynne and Don experienced the power of empathy. It was fun to watch the tension drain away, and the joy of relating enter back into their marriage.

Shifting Into Empathy

I clearly remember the evening my then teenage son, Josh, took me aside for a little "son-father chat."

"What's up, Josh?" I asked innocently.

"I don't think you want me to have fun," he said bluntly.

I looked at him in utter shock. I took a moment to process what he was saying. "You don't want me to have fun," he said. I let the words roll around in my brain.

"I don't understand at all what you mean, Josh," I said. "I want you to enjoy yourself and have the best life imaginable."

"Then why do you criticize me the first thing when you walk into the house. You find something wrong with everything I do. You complain about everything."

I let Josh's words sink in. He was right. I did complain the first thing upon walking into the house. For as much as I wanted to defend my frustration, I could see the pain in his eyes. I felt sad for the pain I was causing him. I now had to look at the problem not only through my eyes, but through his eyes as well. Empathy allows us to do that.

When our children come to us in emotional pain, we know we must set aside everything we're doing and focus on them. We know their pain is front and center. As hard as it might be, we must then validate their emotions, even if we disagree with their point of view. Josh taught me an incredibly valuable lesson.

Years have passed since learning that lesson with Joshua. Out with him one evening this summer, after a strenuous game of tennis, he shared frustration about his long hours at work. As he complained about his work I jumped into Mr. Fix-It mode.

"Why don't you cut back on your hours," I suggested, "so you have more time to do the things you want?"

"It's not that easy," he said, slightly defensive.

"Why not?" I asked.

"They expect me to put in a certain number of hours, and I have little control over it," he said.

"I don't understand," I said, still trying to fix things for him.

"Gosh, Dad," he said. "I don't feel like you're really listening. I know that's a professional hazard of yours, to try to fix things, but I need to know you're really listening to me."

I paused to think about what he was saying. Was I really just trying to fix things? Was I not offering empathy? The longer I paused, the more I could see his point.

"I guess you're right, Josh," I said. "I'm sorry. I hate to see you work so hard, and I can see how hard that is on you. I guess offering quick solutions isn't going to make your life any easier. I'm sorry."

"No worries," he said. "Let me assure you that I'll figure things out."

"Perfect."

After leaving Joshua for the day I realized I had fallen into a pattern of judging what he was saying instead of truly listening. I was jumping to conclusions rather than being open to everything he was saying. I had to reach deep inside to rediscover the power of empathy, which built a bridge to him instead of the narrow thinking that creates distance.

If children feel rejected by a good friend, we listen carefully and share how bad they must feel. If they get bruised physically and consider withdrawing from a school sport, we understand their reluctance and trepidation. We don't force them to move forward before they are ready. The same is true with adults.

I wonder if you can relate with either Lynne and Don, or Josh and me? Consider the possibility that you've been seeing your current problems too narrowly. Is it possible that the people around you just might have something very important to say. Consider, in fact, that *they are totally* **right!** I want to shake you loose from the box you're in. By looking through the eyes of your friends (another way of thinking about empathy) we build a bridge to them. We let go of narrow thinking, learn about them and discover more about ourselves in the process.

So, if your friends were *completely right, unmistakeably right,* what do you need to change? Can you sense the possibilities for your life? Shifting gears isn't always easy. I had to coax Lynne into letting go of her anger temporarily—allowing her room to feel empathy for her husband. She began to sense the power of empathy, and its healing possibilities. She was able to see that he wasn't setting out to frustrate her. He wasn't an insensitive guy trying to create chaos in her world. Far from it. Their work, like yours, requires temporarily putting yourself aside, reaching into another's heart for answers to their questions.

The Power of Empathy

Josh and I are an excellent example of how a lack of empathy pits us against one another, while understanding and empathizing with each other draws us together. When we fully understand each other, and are able to share that empathy effectively, conflict often dissolves. In addition to these positive attributes, empathy also brings you power.

Would your life be calmer if you had more power over the way others react to you? How would you like to determine whether people react to you in a positive, rather than negative way? Learning to relate with empathy can make this happen.

Let's listen in to two different situations at the local hardware store.

Situation One:

CUSTOMER: "I bought this repair kit and it doesn't work the way way it's supposed to. I'd like a refund."

CLERK: "Did you follow the instructions? The mastic only works if you do it according to the instructions."

CUSTOMER: "I know how to use it, and I didn't come in here to get a lecture! I want a refund."

CLERK: "Well, I can't give you a refund. It says right on the box it's non-returnable. You'll have to talk to the manager because that's a non- . . ."

CUSTOMER: "If I'm talking to the manager, it's not going to be about this, it'll be about the $@#$% service in this place. Now give me my refund!"

I bet you can guess where the conversation is going from here. Neither person is going to have a good experience. The clerk's critical approach has triggered a flight or fight response in the customer.

What's happened here is a totally normal brain reaction for the customer. Receptors in his brain recognized a possible threat and shifted brain energy out of the frontal cortex (thinking mode) into brain stem operation (defensive mode.)

We know that when this fight or flight response takes over, the thinking mode shuts down to allow for maximum attack or defense.

Now the customer is, so to speak, a walking brain stem. As a result he blurts out something that immediately turns the clerk into a walking brain stem. So now we have two walking brain stems reacting to each other instead of thinking together.

Let's consider this next scenario:

Situation Two:

CUSTOMER: "I bought this repair kit and it doesn't work the way it's supposed to. I'd like a refund."

CLERK: (leading with empathy) "Oh, no. That's never good. That's got to be frustrating."

CUSTOMER: "You got it. I thought it would work, and now I had to take time to make another trip down here."

CLERK: "Oh, no. Did you notice what it says on the box about it being a non-refundable article? I'll get a manager and see it there is anything we can do for you. Do you have a minute?"

It looks as if this situation is off to a better start. The clerk's use of empathy and/or understanding has managed to keep the customer's brain functioning in thinking mode and avoiding a nasty situation.

But There's a Problem and a Solution

It's great to know we have the power to decide which part of another's brain will be in operation. But being able to unleash that power before we blow the opportunity ourselves can be a problem.

Most of us find we don't have an empathetic thought on the tips our tongues when things are going wrong. Our brains want to and are ready to kick into brain stem operation.

The Secret

It has been discovered that people who do a great job as leaders, often lead with empathy. Their lives seem to be filled with more positive interactions than the average person. These people have learned the secret to reacting with empathy. They know that if they have to think for even a second to come up with an empathetic statement, it's too late. One second, and they revert to what's natural, which can be anything from criticism, to anger, to immediate problem solving.

Here's the secret to they have learned that you may not have picked up yet. They have trained themselves to use one and only one empathetic saying or sound. Keeping this sound or short saying on the tip of the tongue eliminates the need for trying to match empathy to the situation.

Try it. Your co-worker walks in and says he/she overslept and didn't have time for his/her ritual latte. You respond, "That stinks."

Fortunately people are starved for empathy and hearing the same response frequently is not a problem. The brain locks in on the empathy so quickly that it pays little attention to the words instead it locks in on the comforting feeling and the emotional connection that occurs.

The Self-Training Process

Now it's your turn to practice.

Step 1:

Pick an empathetic sound that you like. Be sure that it is one that matches your personality. Be sure that you can say it with true sincerity. There are many effective ones, not limited to:

Wow.
How sad.
Oh, no.
Bless your heart.
What a bummer.
Dang.
That's never good.
An empathetic grunt. (Just the sound.)
Ahaa . . .

Step 2:
Put yourself to sleep at night visualizing responding to someone using your empathetic sound or saying. Plan to do it every night for about 30 days.

EXAMPLE: When James makes me mad, I'm going to say, "Ah . . ."

Step 3:
Pray for the opportunity to run an experiment on someone who gives you a hard time. Think about this over and over as you drive or have time on your hands.

Step 4:
Watch with surprise, the different reactions you get from others as you practice this new skill.

Step 5:
Teach other people how to do the same thing. Your world and theirs will be a much calmer place.

We've looked at how to use the power of empathy to control the way a conversation turns. Now, let's review the power of empathy. As we do, think about your life and how you can apply these principles in your relationships.

Empathy connects people together. We all want to be understood, and the very act of being understood binds people together. It's a basic need.

This is all easier said than done, since most of us want to be understood more than we want to understand. We want to talk more than we want to listen. Sadly, we often want to be right more than we want to really connect to others.

Empathy gets us out of our narrow, rigid point of view and into the other person's world. We listen with the intent to understand. We try to get into their frame of reference. We push aside our own agenda to fully appreciate what is going on in another's mind, and doing this creates an incredibly strong bond.

Try it out. As you empathize with others, you'll feel a new, stronger level of connection.

Empathy heals. When we project our emotions onto others, we remain trapped in our world, isolated and alone. Not only are we alone with our pain, but our friends are alone with theirs.

Again, empathy builds bridges. We enter another's world, walk in their shoes, see things from their perspective. Understanding brings healing. When we receive validation for our point of view, we feel understood. We no longer feel alone.

Empathic listening—listening for the purpose of understanding—is nothing short of magical. I remember a few days ago when I sat down with my wife, Christie, and shared how I had been contacted by an old acquaintance who had hurt me deeply. I shared with her that I was cautious about returning the voicemail he left me, concerned that I could be hurt again. Christie simply listened and empathized with my fears. She indicated that she understood my ambivalance about returning his call, and my trepidation at being hurt again. She didn't try to solve my dilemna, but simply listened empathically.

Why is empathic listening so important? It allows us to feel safe to reveal what we are feeling. We're able to sort out our feelings in the company of someone we know won't judge or condemn us.

Try it out. Remember the empathetic phrase or sound you practiced earlier.

Empathy builds trust. When I sense you care enough about me, and what I'm feeling, and go out of your way to see the world through my eyes, I begin to trust you.

There is a cliché that goes, "I won't care how much you know until I know how much you care." How true. Show me that you care about me and my well-being, and I'm safe with you, and I'll trust you with personal aspects of myself. When we sense others are concerned with our well-being, we place increasing trust in them.

Try it out. Notice how you trust your friends more as they stretch to understand and empathize with your feelings.

Empathy allows you to receive feedback from others. You grow and learn about another when you're really willing to put your agenda aside and listen to them. Although this is so basic, it is incredibly hard to do—especially in an emotional situation.

By keeping your emotions in check, just remembering that secret empathetic sound, you're able to truly focus on someone else. This maintains a powerful bridge of communication. Using empathic listening, you're open to receiving important information. This is information we may not want to hear, but hearing it is critical to our growth.

Try it out. Notice how empathy allows you to listen in new, informative ways. When your friends believe you really care about them, they share more with you. That feels great!

Keeping an Eye Out For Problems

I was amazed to watch the changes between Don and Lynne and Joshua and myself. For such a simple tool, empathy works like rocket fuel in a relationship.

For as potent as empathy is, however, I still have to offer a few warnings. Old behaviors sneak up on us and bite us where we least want to be bitten.

What are the natural barriers to empathic listening? When flooded with his own pain, how does Don empathize with his wife? What about his feelings? How does he get beyond them so he can empathize with his mate? When Lynne is angry, how does she set aside her frustration so she can fully attend to him? There are several barriers to empathy we must recognize and work through.

Emotions: Heightened emotions often get in the way of empathic listening. When I'm absorbed in my own emotional reaction, I can't fully attend to you. When I have an emotional storm brewing inside me, I can't be quiet long enough to be available to you.

Empathic listening requires turning down the volume of my own emotions, in what initially might seem like a detached manner, so I can really be available to you. Even if I can only push my emotions aside temporarily, that gives me the time and ability to tune into you. It takes practice, but it helps in a relationship immensely.

Defensiveness: We often have a tendency to reject what others are saying. Because something about what they are saying is unpleasant, our natural tendency is to shut them out—or up. We want to focus on our feelings. We want to talk about how we've been hurt, not about how we've participated in the hurtful process.

Defensiveness stops us from listening to and empathizing with others. It's like throwing up a wall of bricks and hiding behind it. "Nothing you say is going to get to me," our defensiveness says.

The solution is to be alert to our defensiveness, questioning our reaction. Perhaps we're reacting because we perceive an attack on our ego. Are we feeling old feelings associated with childhood trauma? It could be that we feel fragile and defenseless. Whatever the trigger, we must recognize our defensiveness, tend to it and then set it aside if we're going to empathize with others. Again, having an empathic partner helps.

Resistance: We may not want to listen and learn from others. Absorbed in our own world filled with daily concerns, we may be quite content to stay stuck in our old patterns of relating. We often have blind spots where we've dug our feet, refusing to listen to issues our mate has with us and our marriage.

Healthy relating means remaining open to growth. We must expand our vision, being willing to see and feel more than ever before. We must listen closely to our emotions and others as well. We must recognize that healthy relationships are dynamic places where our weaknesses and failures will eventually be revealed. Expecting that to occur, we're relatively comfortable talking about our human foibles.

Rigid Perceptions: Rigidity perpetuates narrow-mindedness and keeps us stifled. Wherever we think we know it all, we're closed to receiving new information. Any time we refuse to consider new information, our relationships suffer.

Being empathic to others means considering the value of their point of view, even if it differs from ours. We are able to 'be with' their position, and hope they can 'be with' ours. Sharing different points of view is part of what makes relating exciting.

Empathy opens up incredible new horizons. Empathy allows us to fully appreciate what it's like to walk in the shoes of someone else. We see through their eyes. We feel what they feel. We understand what is important to them.

Arrogance: Arrogance breeds a condescending spirit, which kills empathy. Arrogance, by definition, is believing you are "above" another person, leaving you unable to fully empathize with them. Have you ever noticed how much you distrust someone who believes they know it all, or lets you know they would never do what you've done, or could feel what you feel. We tend to distance ourselves from people like that.

Empathy, however, brings us closer to one another. When empathizing with another we begin to recognize our similiaries, as opposed to our differences. We notice the humanness in their actions, and realize we too are fully capable of anything they have said or done. No one is better than another.

Empathy is an incredibly powerful tool that draws us together. True empathy says, "I can relate to what you're going through because of my experiences." We're all really in the same boat. That's the beauty of empathy. I hope you are as excited about this tool as I am. It works.

Vulnerability

Are you beginning to feel the power of these *Love and Logic* principles? They're not just for kids anymore. They're nothing fancy, just good old-fashioned common sense.

There is one more aspect of empathy we all must understand to really appreciate its power—*empathy involves vulnerability.* You cannot empathize with someone, or have them empathize with you, without vulnerability. Talking to the people in your life on their level, letting them know you understand what they're experiencing, allows you to be vulnerable with them. Vulnerability is the oomph behind intimacy—or "into me see." By tearing down the barriers of *emotionality, defensiveness, resistance, rigid perceptions* and *arrogance*, we are emotionally naked. We sit before another in our most vulnerable state—without pretense. "What you see is what you get."

I had a wonderful discussion with my youngest son, Tyson, recently as he shared how the rigors of medical school had taken their toll on him. (I'd learned some powerful lessons from my discussions with his brother Josh) Tyson felt stressed, tense and anxious, to the point of it effecting his sleep.

I was transported back to my graduate studies, and how, for a time, I wondered if I could complete that program. I felt his vulnerability, sharing how I struggled with anxiety at times as well. Being a psychologist, I often felt (unrealistically) that I should never feel anxious, that I should have the answers to any emotional problem. He empathized with me, relating that medical school taught that he, too, should have all the answers.

Far from being an awkward moment of transparency, our vulnerability with each other brought us closer. I thanked Tyson for trusting me enough to share his challenge with me, and silently I thanked Josh for challenging me. In this poignant moment, our empathy drew us closer. No longer separated by years or our father-son relationship, we were two people with similar emotions and experiences.

Run This Experiment

Now it's your turn. It's time to add the power of empathy to the other tools you've collected. It's time to run an experiment—and you know how much we like running experiments. Remember, some of these tools are going to work naturally and effectively, while others may take a bit longer to master. Nothing ventured, nothing gained.

Here it is: During the next conversation with a sibling or best friend, simply empathize. Just listen, occasionally uttering an empathetic word, phrase or sound, and learn more about what he/she is saying. Ask questions and reflect that you understand. Say back to them what you heard them say, suggesting you've had similar experiences if that is the case.

Watch for them to indicate that you're getting what they are trying to communicate. Don't offer an opinion, or react emotionally. If they're saying something critical to you, don't react. Make an empathetic sound, and just listen.

Again, in one, two, three, four fashion:

1. Listen
2. Learn
3. Validate
4. Empathize

Do you notice a positive bridge between you? Pay attention to the warm, fuzzy feeling of connection. This is the real juice of relating. Empathy is a powerful tool you can carry with you for every relationship.

Having experimented with neutralizing arguments, delaying consequences and empathizing, you're now ready to add yet another powerful tool to your tool box: *setting enforceable consequences*. Let's keep moving forward and see how this tool fits in with the ones you've already learned.

4

Setting Limits With Enforceable Consequences

"Healthy boundaries let you choose who you allow into your space and how they treat you. Healthy boundaries help you figure out who you are—an individual separate from everyone else—and what treatment you'll accept."
—Laurie Pawlik-Klenien

Human beings work hard to make things difficult. Life, however, is pretty simple. Everything I need to know I really did learn in kindergarten—or from my grandmother.

Perhaps the thing I love the most about *Love and Logic* principles is they're so simple. They're based on everyday, practical principles easily applied to everyday life.

But, back to kindergarten and my grandmother.

I still remember some of the powerful lessons of kindergarten:

- Wait your turn—or lose it.
- Be nice to others—or sit in the corner alone.
- Clean up your messes—or miss playtime.
- Raise your hand if you want to talk—or sit quietly.
- No swearing—or get your mouth washed out with soap. (I know I'm dating myself on that one.)

My grandmother must have talked to my kindergarten teacher, because they did things the same way. I still hear my grandmother's voice:

> *"David. When you finish your dinner we can make paste and cut things out of magazines."*
> *"David. You may play with us when you leave other people's things alone."*
> *"David. We will be willing to listen when you use your indoor voice."*

My grandmother and kindergarten teacher were, of course, brilliant. Without knowing it, they were practicing the principle we're now going to apply to our adult relationships: *setting limits with enforceable consequences*.

Looking back over the things my teacher and grandmother told me, I see statements that attached enforceable consequences to certain specific behaviors. In a nutshell, if I was nice, I could count on being able to join in the fun. If I wasn't, life wouldn't look so good and I'd find myself sitting alone and left out of the fun. From kindergarten and Grandma, I learned my first valuable lessons in cause and effect connections.

Lessons Learned the Hard Way

As simple and brilliant as my teacher's and grandmother's lessons were, it is amazing how quickly I forgot them. As soon as I became a parent I went brain dead, forgetting those lessons about cause and effect. I forgot the invaluable lesson of *setting limits with enforceable consequences*. Can you relate?

Parenthood was not easy—no instruction manual and loads of responsibilities. A perfect scenario for disaster.

While becoming a parent was incredibly exciting, I was dumbstruck with the responsibility. There were many things about being a parent I hated. I hated it when my sons bickered with each other, and I felt powerless to stop it. I hated it when they pouted at the dinner table, and again felt powerless to stop it. I hated it when they had to be cajoled, tricked or bribed into practicing their piano lessons. I especially hated having to repeatedly stop them from wearing my gym socks. (Okay, the last one seems incredibly petty now, but let me tell you, it seemed worth fighting about at the time.) Nothing I did stopped the endless pattern of them disobeying me, and me getting annoyed and angry.

There was one thing however, that seemed to help me feel powerful—act tough and yell. When all else failed, I always knew I was bigger than my children and could force them into action. While hardly a model form of parenting, and definitely not in the arsenal of the *Love and Logic* parent, brawn came in handy when brains were in short supply.

But we're playing in a different arena now—this world of using *Love and Logic* tools in our adult relationships. Thankfully, the same tools used by our grandmothers and kindergarten teachers are going to help us with our challenging adult relationships. Our opponent however, is no whiny two-year-old or testy four-year-old. We're now matching wits with someone with an ego as large as ours, and the willpower to prove it.

Thankfully it doesn't take the brains of a rocket scientist—which I don't have—or the brawn of Mike Tyson—which I'm also short on, to use these tools in our adult relationships. What our relationships do require is a bit of mental toughness and resolve. It's all about *setting limits with enforceable consequences*. It's about understanding what is important to you and the boundaries you set up to protect those core values, that drive your limit-setting. You can be sure a boundary has been violated if you find yourself becoming resentful about the same things, time and again. Those are the places that need close attention.

You're going to see how easy it is to practice, in much the same way we do with children, to be clear about boundaries and then attach limits to them. Pairing limits with boundaries that are important to us, is what this chapter is all about. You're going to be amazed at how valuable this particular tool is when it comes to relating with the meaningful people in your world.

Going Blank

Even though setting limits can be simple, most of us don't do it. Though it is one of the sharpest tools in our toolbox, we leave it sitting idle, unused. We do this by "going blank," forgetting we own this powerful tool. We allow ourselves to be stunned, shocked, alarmed and perhaps even outraged—all emotions that cause us to "forget" we are strong, powerful and have a wonderful tool ready for use.

Just the other day I encountered this problem in a counseling session—a woman who went "blank" in response to her friend's behavior. In this particular example, a forty-year-old woman named Jessica came to my office in a state of panic, completely perplexed about what she could possibly do with her girlfriend, who refused to change her behavior. I let her complain for several minutes, listening to a sad story I'd heard many times.

"You won't believe what happened to me," she complained. "My friend, Kelly, calls me time and again, ranting and raving about her angry husband."

"Tell me about your relationship with her," I suggested.

"Oh, we've been best friends for years, and I like her a lot. But, she keeps getting herself into these messes with her husband and other people around her and then calls me up to complain."

"Okay," I said, "and then what?"

"Well, I want to be her friend, and care about her, but I'm tired of listening to issue after issue," she said softly.

"You sound tired," I said empathically. "I can imagine caring about your friend, but also getting weary of being her sounding board all the time. So, how do you set limits on her complaining?"

Although I hear it regularly, her response surprised me.

"Well, sometimes I tell her what to do, but she doesn't really listen to me," she said meekly. "Mostly I've learned to just keep my mouth shut. I don't think she takes me seriously anyway."

"No," I said. "That's pretty obvious, isn't it? She doesn't seem to take you seriously at all, and I wonder if she even respects what you say. You've got to feel furious inside."

"I suppose," she continued. "But, I just get confused and can't think straight. I listen to story after story, and get more and more annoyed. I don't know what to do. That's why I'm here."

"I'm going to help you not go blank," I said reassuringly. "In fact, we're going to talk about coming alive, instead of going blank. We're going to talk about knowing what you think, boundaries you want to set and how exactly you want to act with your friend."

"I'd like that," she said. "I really hope you can help me."

I most certainly could help Jessica, and can help you as well. But, help comes in the form of change, and change means we must give up our old ways of doing things in favor of more effective ways.

Would it surprise you to know that Jessica is a very bright woman? In fact, she is so bright that she is vice president of one of our local banks. Does that surprise you? It shouldn't, because there is really no connection between "going blank" and running banks. You can be a NASA super-scientist, sending men and women to the moon, and still "blank out" when it comes to setting limits with those around you.

Have I piqued your curiosity about how you too can move from "blanking out," and feeling hopeless, to a place with limits, boundaries, power and influence?

Getting Smart

We are already smart people, and we're going to get even smarter. Remember, these tools are simple. They were crafted in kindergarten classes and grandmothers' kitchens. We've been able to get smart since the beginning of time, and thankfully it's never too late to learn new skills. So, are you ready to get smart—or smarter?

Sitting with Jim Fay over a cup of coffee, he shared that the incredible strengths of *Love and Logic* is the power to get kids (and adults!) to think—in short, to get smart.

"So, how do you do that, Jim?" I asked. "Especially when both kids and adults give you that look that says they don't have a clue what you're talking about?"

Jim gave one of those hearty laughs he is famous for.

"Easy," he said. "But, you do have to be a little cagey."

"Cagey?" I asked, watching him lean back in his chair.

"Sure," he said. "We act pretty dumb sometimes, when we're not. We let kids, and adults, get away with so much and then complain about what happens. We set kids and adults up to rebel against us, when we could use a little magic to get them to cooperate with us."

"Okay, so what's the magic tool?"

"It's a special blend of two powerful techniques, sincere empathy and natural consequences," he said. "Each of these, on their own, has their own special power, but when we combine them the blend becomes extraordinary.

"Actually, what we've found with kids is that when we pair empathy with consequences, we pack a powerful one-two punch. If it works with kids it can work with adults too."

Jim went on to share the following examples: For the kid who forgets his lunch at home, and now faces a cafeteria full of hungry kids chomping down their lunch, you can be sure his empty stomach is a rude reminder to remember his lunch. For the kid who forgets to clean her room and has to tell her friends that she cannot come out to play, she learns the importance of cleaning her room before going out to play.

Compare these situations. Which one causes the child to be angry with the adult? Which one forces the child to do some heavy duty thinking?

Situation one:

"Shannon. You know that throwing food in the cafeteria is against the rules. I'm tired of telling you about this. I'm suspending you from the cafeteria for a week. I hope that teaches you a good lesson!"

Situation two:

"Oh, wow, Shannon. This is really sad. Throwing food again. Where are you going to be eating your lunch now that you can't be in the cafeteria for the next week?"

Now let's move this idea into the world of adults.

Here's the set-up:

"Marge. Can you believe that the same cop gave me another ticket? I wasn't going any faster than the rest of the traffic and he singled me out again."

Situation one:

"Dan, I told you that you are going to have to slow down. I don't know why you don't pay better attention. You're just going to have to pay for that ticket out of your golf money. I'm not taking it out of the household budget this time!"

Situation two:

"Oh, Dan, that's got to be so frustrating. I hope the insurance company is as understanding as I am. Give me a hug and come to dinner."

As you can see, the same cause-effect sequence can have powerful effects with adults as well. For the man who forgets his dinner date with his girlfriend, and then has to eat a cold dinner alone, you can be sure he'll feel the impact. For the woman who overspends her checking account and receives an overdraft notice, and must tell her roommates she's going to be late with the rent, you can be sure she will feel that impact.

Consequences have an amazing ability to make us smart, quickly. They help us think before we act, and remember the repercussion of our actions. They help us look before we leap; think before we act; prepare before we launch into an endeavor.

Do these same principles really work with adults? What do you think? A couple of years ago, when I was in the habit of speeding, I discovered they work powerfully. One sunny afternoon I sped around the corner in my Volkswagen bug with the top down, enjoying some tunes. Caught up in the moment, I didn't notice the police car tucked off the roadway. Although I didn't notice him, he noticed me.

Soon my delightful mood was shattered by an officer who wrote me a ticket for speeding. No amount of pleading could convince the officer not to give me the ticket.

"You need to watch your speed, Sir," he said in his officious voice. No doubt.

I decided to learn my lesson, to get smart. However, no sooner had the pain of that ticket passed when several weeks later I received yet another ticket. Unbelievable! This time the officer was even less sympathetic. Scolding me loudly, he handed me another ticket.

Cussing under my breath, I decided this would never happen again. I vacillated between being angry at the officer for catching me, and my own stupid actions. I reviewed the cost of another ticket, and how I would explain my actions to my wife. But, this was not the end of my sad saga.

Not two months later I received my third speeding ticket. Don't ask me how I could be so dumb. Don't ask me what I was thinking. Don't ask me anything because I have no answers, other than to say I "went blank." I stopped thinking. I failed to anticipate consequences, yet again.

That third ticket with its "invitation" to attend Drivers Education classes broke through my denial and ignorance, simply telling me: "David, if you want to drive in the future, you will learn a lesson. The lesson comes with a price tag of taking drivers education classes, higher insurance payments along with the threat of losing your license."

I angrily participated in the Drivers Education classes. I angrily paid the fines and higher insurance premiums. Most important, I taped the letter from the Washington State Department of Motor Vehicles to my dash. It stayed there for a year—long enough for me to learn a lesson about driving, consequences and responsibility.

Do consequences work? You bet they do. Do consequences teach invaluable lessons? No question about it. Consequences have a way of waking us up, breaking through our denial and ignorance, causing us to think, think, and think again. Using consequences creates an ingenious method for me to "get smart."

Jessica Getting Smart

What do I mean by *getting smart?* It means thinking about the behaviors that are driving you stark raving mad, considering the new limits you want so those behaviors don't continue, and pairing enforceable consequences to them. It's that simple to *get smart*.

I enjoy helping all kinds of adults get smart in the ways they interact with their mates and friends. Painful lessons are learned because of consequences, and this powerful *Love and Logic* tool will empower you to get smarter in your adult relationships. You never have to go blank again. You never have to be treated with disrespect again.

Remember Jessica from earlier in the chapter? Like many others, she was caught in an endless cycle of violated boundaries, feeling powerless and discouraged. Actually, because her boundaries didn't have consequences attached to them, they weren't really boundaries at all. I helped her create enforceable limits, increasing her self-confidence in her relationships.

Jessica and I explored ways she could become strong and powerful just by learning to *set limits with enforceable consequences*. We started by creating real boundaries, such as refusing to listen to her friend's endless complaining. She shared how she was happy to listen to her friend's concerns as long as they were also talking about solutions. She set limits on how often and how long she could talk to her friend. She discovered her friend responding to her boundaries, and in fact came to enjoy their conversations.

Jessica became almost giddy at the simplicity and power of this tool. She had been ready to make some steps to improve her friendship, and this tool would help her, but it took some work. Change never comes easily.

Here was her recipe for change, and it can work for you as well:

First, *take inventory of your situation*. Instead of being repeatedly taken off guard, you must assess your situation. What are the behaviors that are intolerable? In fact, I call them the *intolerables*. What *must* change? Not the things you wish would change, but the things that *must* change. Anything you put on the list must be something you are ready to get tough about.

Jessica decided she would not spend hours on the phone with her friend complaining about her life. She decided their conversations had to include talking about solutions for her to feel useful. She also decided they must also talk about her life, and not only her friend's.

Now it's your turn. Make a list of those behaviors that are intolerable. Determine what must change. I've learned an invaluable motto you might want to memorize: *a boundary without consequences is not a boundary, but is a wish or a hope*. Most often we slip into complaining, which is a sure sign that your boundaries are not being enforced. You must be willing to take decisive action on those behaviors you decide are intolerable. If you simply wish they would change without you taking any action, don't put them on your list.

Second, *attach consequences to these behaviors*. You don't need to know what those consequences are at this point. Be strong enough to say to yourself, "I will not tolerate this behavior any longer, and am willing to consider consequences to those behaviors."

Can you feel the strength in your resolve? You don't need to have all the answers yet. (Remember the tool of *delaying consequences?*) The answers will come. It is enough for now to *come alive, get smart, become alert and strong*.

Jessica decided she was ready for change. She could see that the starting point for change was not with her friend, but with herself. She had to create sharp edges that form boundaries. She had to think over each issue, brainstorming possible consequences.

Third, *prepare for change*. Some very bright psychologists have found that making any kind of change to a situation changes behavior. In other words, if you simply stop doing what you've been doing when faced with an intolerable behavior, you're on the right track.

For Jessica, this meant that shutting down wasn't working for her, and, in fact, this behavior only enabled Kelly to keep treating her the same. Becoming quiet reinforced her friend's behavior. She discovered her voice and began speaking up, which was a powerful beginning for her.

Jessica also had to explore her own anxiety about change. For as much as she wanted things to change, she had to recognize part of her wanted to keep quiet, ignoring the problems. There was some strange safety in keeping things the same—but, now she was ready for change.

Fourth, *prepare for resistance to your actions*. Don't expect everyone to applaud when you say, "I'm not taking this anymore." Your friends may even laugh when you announce the idea of consequences to actions. That's okay. As you share your ideas and the possibilities in this book, they'll eventually see the wisdom of these tools.

"Yeah, right," might be the first response you hear. So, don't get all excited that people will cheer you on. Be prepared to go the first part of the journey alone, and with resistance. That's okay. You can do it. Pushing against resistance makes you stronger.

Kelly had complained and whined to Jessica their entire relationship, and she needed to prepare herself as she changed. Kelly might become irritated, ignore her, or possibly even become angrier. She had to anticipate all possible consequences.

Finally, *attach consequences to behavior*. Yes, this is possibly the hardest part of the game, but you can do it. This is where you get tough. This is where you draw a line in the sand—Announcement: If you go beyond this point, be prepared to face some stiff consequences. Like my Kindergarten teacher said, "If you don't wait your turn, be prepared to lose it."

In each of these examples, you can see the power of the enforceable consequences. Threats, made over and over without enforceable consequences, hold no power or impact.

Here are some ideas of what the "old Jessica" might have done, and what the "new Jessica" might do:

The old Jessica might have said:

"I can't understand why you put up with so much from your husband. You've got to stop it." (unenforceable)

The new Jessica, armed with the tool of setting enforceable limits with consequences said, *"I'll be happy to talk to you, Kelly, but I must limit my listening to your relationship to your husband to just a few minutes."* (enforceable)

"I hate what you put yourself through, and you need to get control of yourself." (unenforceable)

"I know, Kelly, that you will set limits on your brother when you're ready. But, I can only listen to your concerns for a few minutes." (enforceable)

"You have got to change, Kelly. You must make it safe for me to share feedback with you." (unenforceable)

"I'll share my feedback with you when I feel it is respected." (enforceable)

For some of you these actions may seem very scary. You wonder if you're really up for this challenge. Yes, you are. Yes, you must be. While change is never easy, it is the only path to healthier living. You can do it.

The Three A's

For the same price I'm throwing in a "bonus" tool. I simply couldn't help myself and am excited to share this one because it fits in so nicely with *setting limits with enforceable consequences.*

This really isn't new, since most of us grew up with parents demanding that we apologize, acknowledge the wrongfulness of our actions and make some sort of gesture showing we really meant business. I've taken these principles one step further and woven them into the powerful strategy from this chapter.

You now know how to set limits with enforceable consequences. You know how to set boundaries, and to add consequences to violations of those boundaries. Now, consider this:

With every significant violation—and I mean *every significant violation!*—the violator must—and I do mean *must*—perform *The Three A's.* (For simple infractions a sincere apology may suffice.) But, for Significant Infractions, these three additional tools help change behavior:

- *Apologize*—The violator must offer a sincere apology for his/her actions. This is a very logical consequence of wronging someone. When wronging someone, we expect to have to apologize, and when wronged, we want a sincere apology.
- *Accept Responsibility*—The violator must take full responsibility for his/her actions. The violator must understand the impact his/her behavior has on you, and the ripple effect of those actions. Expressing any understanding of the wrongfulness of our actions is a powerful bridge to the one we've hurt (remember the power of empathy).
- *Amends*—The violator offers to do something for you that meaningfully makes up for the harm he/she has caused. This might be as simple as sharing a heartfelt apology, or as complex as reading a book on relationships. The bottom line is that the amends must fit the violation, and show they are sincere in our efforts to change.

Let's consider what this might look like look in a situation where your friend continuously oversteps her bounds. Let's say your friend repeatedly takes you for granted. You loan her money—she takes her time in paying it back. You go out of your way to perform favors for her—she rarely reciprocates. You call her to find out how she's doing—she doesn't check in with you to see how you are doing.

Having read this chapter, you learned to *set limits with enforceable consequences.* But, she still pushes the limits. Things reach a boiling point when your friend borrows a significant sum of money when in trouble, promising to pay you back. But, she's gone well past the deadline and you're fuming.

How would *the Three A's* help you?

You screw up your courage, review *the Three A's* and make the phone call:

"Gloria," you say firmly. "I'm calling because you haven't paid back the money you promised."

"Uh, yeah, I've had some hard times," she mutters. "I'll get it to you as soon as I can."

"This is hard for me to say," you continue, "but, that won't be good enough. I need something more from you in addition to the money."

"What do you mean?" she asks.

"You have really put me out this time," you say emphatically. "This has happened before and a promise to repay me won't be enough to make our friendship right, which I hope is important to you."

"Of course it is," she says. "I don't want you to take this personally."

"Well I do take it personally," you say. "So for me to be okay with you I need three things: a sincere apology, your letting me know you understand how your actions have damaged our friendship, and not only repaying the money, but doing something special for me to make up for the trouble you've caused me."

You hear your friend gasp as you wait anxiously for their response.

"Um, well I didn't think it was that big of a deal," she says.

"It is that big of a deal," you say, "and I need you to take it as a big deal."

"I guess that's reasonable," she says reluctantly. "I do value our friendship and will make things right. I'm sorry for the trouble I've caused you, I feel embarrassed and will not only repay you, but will think of something special to do to make things right between us."

"That would be nice," you say, "and as soon as that is done, we can be friends again."

Does this sound harsh? At times it may feel that way. But remember, *a boundary without consequences is not a boundary.* You *must* be prepared for resistance. You must anticipate a challenge and you must follow through with consequences. You calmly, clearly look at the person and tell him or her you will not act as if nothing is wrong. Positive behavior leads to positive consequences. Repeated violations of boundaries lead to tough consequences.

How might *the Three A's* look in a marital violation where one partner has taken advantage of another repeatedly? While the relationship is broken—before *the Three A's* have been performed, there might be no dinners together, no smiles or hugs. Certainly no sex. The relationship is broken until *the Three A's* are enforced—and this leads to a lot of motivation to act positively.

Now some folks wonder if they always need to perform *the Three A's*. Are there situations where two of the A's might be enough? Yes! Might one A be enough? Of course. Remember the rule that there are no hard and fast rules. Try things out. See which ones fit and discard the rest.

And what if *the Three A's* have little effect on the troubling behavior? The Third A may need to be intensified—meaningful consequences must change behavior. If they don't, the violator isn't taking things seriously enough. That's the principle! But again—experiment with this. See what works for you.

Respect Established

Please don't expect everything to immediately fall into place once you begin employing these tools in your relationship. Every change brings with it a little chaos. Your mate, employee, friend or family member may want to scream, "What is this? What is this new behavior? I don't recognize it, and furthermore, I don't like it!"

You cannot automatically expect people to respect you, especially when the behavior is new to them. Even our kindergarten teachers, mothers and grandmothers had to demand respect. They had to set limits with enforceable consequences and so do you.

Consequences, boundaries and *the Three A's* all scream R-E-S-P-E-C-T. Together they create structure in a relationship so everyone knows what can be expected. It is your responsibility to create this structure, with these clear boundaries, so the people in your world know what to expect.

If you treat me this way, you can expect this to happen. Can you sense the respect woven into the relationship? It's been said we teach people how to treat us, and these tools will clearly and convincingly teach people they must treat you with respect.

Run This Experiment

It's your turn again—time for an experiment, and this is going to be fun. It's time to put this new tool into practice and notice what works, and what doesn't. Remember, not every tool works the same way with each person, and that's why we call it an experiment.

So, here's what we want you to do. Take a close look at the steps listed below.

1. Consider your life. Is there one situation troubling you where you could begin practicing the tools of this chapter?
2. Determine to set a limit with enforceable consequences.
3. Expect some resistance to your actions.
4. Prepare for discomfort as you begin to change.
5. Attach a consequence to a behavior you want changed.

Try it. Test it. Tweak it. Don't expect things to work perfectly, but watch to see what is effective and what is not. You can expect powerful results.

Okay. Now that we've worked on neutralizing arguments, delaying consequences empathizing and setting limits with enforceable consequences, could there be anything left to learn? As a matter of fact, yes. There is more and these tools are equally powerful. You're now ready to learn our next tool: *guiding others to solve their own problems.*

5

Encouraging Others to Solve Their Own Problems

"I can't solve my own problems, but I sure want to solve yours."

—ANONYMOUS

Okay. Let's take a short break and retrace our steps, a little like Hansel and Gretel placing crumbs on the trail to make sure they can find their way back home. It's not like we're lost or anything, but we do want to back up every so often to remember everything we're learning. This is powerful stuff, and the more we practice, learn, practice, learn, the healthier our relationships are going to be.

So, let's see . . . we've learned:

- the power of neutralizing arguments—this one's super-powerful;
- the importance of delaying consequences—always good to take a breath, think and consider our choices;
- how to unleash the power of empathy—the ability to feel another's emotions, creating a powerful connection to them;
- setting limits with enforceable consequences—a boundary without consequences is not a boundary, but a hope, wish or pie-in-the-sky dream.

If you stop here, which we hope you don't, you'll have gotten a lot from this book. But, we've got even more power-packed tools for your toolkit. Our next tool, sure to help you solve many interpersonal problems, is *encouraging and supporting others to solve their own problems*.

When I was a kid I played a game called 'Pick Up Sticks.' I'm not sure what was so incredible about that game, if you can even call it a game. The instructions called for dumping out a tin of toothpick-like colored sticks and then picking them up, one at a time, without disrupting the rest of the sticks. Of course this was next to impossible.

Problems can be like that bundle of sticks on the floor, each issue intertwines with other issues. Bundled together in a murky mess and packed tightly in a brain, and you've got what many of us face every day—a gob of emotional stuff jumbled together. Try to pick just one to work on and you're sure to mess up the whole pile.

Now, add another aspect to this picture. Imagine someone else mucking around in your brain, trying to "help" you pick out one issue to solve. Imagine someone close to you pronouncing themselves Expert—having *all* the answers, ready and willing to tell you what to do with your life. Finally, imagine them doing all of this *without your permission!*

If this scene causes you to shudder, you're getting the picture. That's why you've got to have our next powerful tool—*encouraging other to solve their own problems*. We'll explain why it's so important for getting along.

I'm already hearing the murmuring of some of you who really do believe you can not only solve your problems, but those of your friends, family and everyone else. Armed with a sense of self-importance, you have perfected The Art of Giving Advice. You've talked yourself into thinking that even though you're overwhelmed at times with your own problems, you can somehow set your issues aside, roll up your sleeves, and reach into another's brain like a skilled neurosurgeon.

This sense of grandiosity is common to all of us at times, and leads to lots of problems. The belief that we have the answers for others not only takes us away from leading our own lives, but diminishes others' capabilities as well. Assuming we have the answers for others, challenges their dignity, and that's something we never want to do—and they probably don't want us to.

The *Love and Logic* founders strongly believe that each child, as well as adult, is armed with the tools or can learn the tools, to solve their own problems. Jim Fay and Foster Cline maintain that we must embrace the dignity of every individual, and that includes their right to manage their life. Since this principle is so effective with kids, let's see if it works as well with adults.

Why is this principle of self-control and dignity so important for kids, small and large? Like our other tools, this one is powerful and can really be magical in helping you relate effectively with every one in your life.

While visiting Jim Fay at his home in Colorado, he shared this story:

My daughter, Nancy, was a very bright child who loved to learn. She taught herself to read when she was only four years old. Needless to say that caused her some concerns when she was in first grade because she finished her assignments quickly and had to wait for the others to finish.

It wasn't long before she came home complaining to Shirley and me that she was bored and wanted us to tell the teacher to do something to solve the problem.

Shirley and I started to fear that if she thought it was the teacher's job to keep her from being bored, she would soon believe it was her parent's job to keep her stimulated. We thought it would be best if she grew up believing her own happiness was her job, not the responsibility of others.

Our discussion with Nancy played out this way:

"Nancy, it's really sad that you are so bored at school. What do you think you are going to do?

"I don't know."

"Gee, that's a double problem, being bored and not knowing what to do. Would you like to hear what some other kids have tried?

"I guess so."

"Well, let's see. Some kids talk to the other kids while they are waiting. How do you think that would work out?

"The teacher would get mad and I'd be in trouble.

"Yeah, I guess so. Well, some kids complain to the teacher. How do you think that might work out?

"I don't think she'd like that."

"Yeah, I guess so. Well, some kids ask the teacher if there might be some other things they could do to help the teacher while they are waiting. How do you think that would work out?

"I don't know."

"Well sweetie, we've run out of ideas. I guess if anyone were going to find a way to deal with this, it would probably be you. Good luck. I hope it works out for you."

Needless to say, this wasn't what Nancy was looking for. She just looked at us like we were from some other planet. We felt like we were letting her down big time. Over breakfast, Shirley and I discussed the possibility of going to school to discuss this with the teacher.

That afternoon Nancy came home wearing a big smile, saying, "I talked to the teacher and asked her if I could go to the library to read some of the big books when I finished my work, and I got to go there two times today!" Problem solved.

Years later, Nancy was a freshman at college. We got the call. "Dad, I'm bored with college."

Remember the success from the first grade experience, I replied, "Well, Nancy. What have you done in the past to solve that kind of problem?"

"Oh, Dad. I know. My happiness is my job. I'll work it out."

It wasn't long before we got a call from Nancy telling us that the solu-

tion she came up with was to carry a double major. As you can guess,
Nancy has been a problem solver throughout her entire life.

Everyone is Capable

All relationships are built on the self-esteem of the individuals.
Just as we want our children to be solid in their individuality, our
adult relationships work best if everyone in the relationships has a
strong sense of self. Let me show you how this works.

My wife Christie, is a unique person. She is lively, enthusiastic
and fun-loving, as well as being just a bit distractible. She loves
jumping from one wonderful idea to another. She's a great 'starter'
of ideas, and not the best 'finisher.' At times this drives me crazy.

While I (David) am also distractible, I tend toward being over-
focused. When I find a project I like, I want to push fast and hard
to completion. I want everyone around me to work just as hard
and fast as I do.

Perhaps you can already guess that we have tension when it
comes to cooperating on a project. Who is right about the pace of
a project? Neither of us. Christie must respect my energy and de-
termination, and I must respect her deliberate, but more subdued
pace. As we value each other, reinforcing our strengths, we work
compatibly. Our individuality and self-esteem is reinforced. If we
expect the other to behave as we do, we've got trouble.

Things didn't go smoothly recently.

"Why aren't you calling back on that interior design referral?" I
asked her recently, feeling a sense of impatience.

"I'm waiting until I get my measurements together," she responded with a hint of irritation.

"But, I thought that was going to happen at the first of the
week," I continued, bolting past her subtle boundary.

"I'm going to take care of things at my own pace," she said, now
clearly upset with me. "I need to run my business my way—not
your way."

Now I got it. She reminded me that we do things differently, and made a special note to give me the following important message: *I am fully capable of managing my life.*

What a lesson. We are all fully capable of managing our lives, as much as we might want to think otherwise. With a bit of encouragement, we are able to figure out what we need to do to become a success. We are able to find the resources we need to become a success.

This, of course, goes against everything we've been taught. If you're like me, you function on the following premises:

- *Everyone* needs my help.
- *Everyone* will mess up their life if given enough time and liberty.
- *Everyone* **falsely** believes they know what they're doing.
- *I must* offer help whenever possible—and that will fix things.

These beliefs get us into huge trouble. These beliefs create stress between Christie and me. These false notions create undue dependence between me and the people I counsel. These beliefs are incredible putdowns and cause insecurity in my relationships.

Why is that? Because strength is gained by developing our muscles, whether it comes to physical strength or mental strength. We know what we need to grow, and simply need encouragement to try out our ideas. If we fail, we learn much more. I learned this lesson the hard way many years ago.

Sometime during my twenties I decided I wanted to be a gentleman farmer. I lived in the country on five acres and had room to roam and dream about what a farmer might do. I decided to dive in. I set out to do all the things a farmer does: till a plot of ground for a garden; purchase some cows; obtain a couple of dogs; build a chicken coop. The only thing missing now were the chickens.

With visions of farm-fresh eggs in my mind I decided to start my chicken-raising business from scratch. I purchased a single hen and rooster, collected the eggs, and set out to incubate them. With the incubator set at just the right temperature and humidity, I held the eggs up to the light daily, revealing growing embryos. Delighted, I took pride in being a real farmer.

As the embryos grew into chicks, they began to peck at their shells, anxious to 'break free.' In my excitement, I decided to give the chicks a helping hand, cutting away the shells to allow them freedom. I couldn't wait for the fluffy balls of fuzz to begin their peeping. No sooner had I cut away their shells, however, than these fluffy balls began acting faint. They couldn't stand, and in fact, died one by one. Horrified, I sought answers to what happened. I discovered the chicks needed to peck their own way out in order to gain strength for their journey. They needed to solve their own problem, and my help killed them.

Self-esteem is gained much the same way—kids and adults need to figure out their own problems. They need to stretch their brains to develop strength for their ongoing journey. We rescue them at their peril. While we may tell ourselves we are being helpful, this is most often not the case. We handicap them and may even cause emotional damage.

Temptation to Rescue

It's very tempting to rescue others. Seeing them as helpless and needing us, we reach into their lives and muck around. We fumble with others' 'pick up sticks' of problems and tell ourselves we're providing invaluable help. *We're not!*

We have a nearly insatiable temptation to rescue others. Some of us have never seen a problem we aren't tempted to fix. We get something of a high out of peering into our friends' lives and offering ways they can do something better.

Just the other day my wife had lunch with a friend. Kate is a winsome, energetic woman who recently retired from teaching. They've known each other for years and have many things in common.

The problem came up when Kate shared some problems she was having with her grown daughter.

Kate began their conversation by complaining:

"My daughter, Nicole, only calls me when she wants something. Blah, blah, blah."

Before she knew it Christie jumped in, offering all kinds of advice on how to handle the situation.

"Maybe you can do this . . ."

Before lunch was over, both Christie and Kate were exhausted from their blah, blah, blahs, and yadda, yadda, yaddas. Neither feeling anything but frustration. How would it have looked if Christie had used the tool of "encouraging others to solve their own problem?"

"Kate, I'm hearing how difficult this is for you right now. But, I've seen you handle similar situations effectively before, and you know how best to handle things with Nicole. You know how to take care of yourself and set healthy boundaries with her."

While Kate may have initially wanted more, she would also feel uplifted by Christie's encouragement. Moreover, she would be empowered to solve her own problem, lessening her dependency on others to fix things for her. It's a win-win solution.

The Meddling Mother Triangle

There are many mothers who cannot stop mothering, no matter how old or grown up their children are—or how old they are! Mothers often operate with an unspoken rule that they are allowed and have permission to "mother" their children forever. This, of course, doesn't sit well with many 'kids.' Furthermore, as we've said, this doesn't allow 'kids' to learn and grow up.

One young couple counseled with me about this issue. The husband, Kerry, had a strong relationship with his mother. It was so strong that for the first years of his marriage he called his mother on a regular basis to inform her about his marriage and business life. This seemed to be a natural part of his functioning. It wasn't until his wife, Darla, challenged him that he began to question his relationship to his mother as well.

"It seems like he can't do anything without checking it out with his mother," she said. "Don't get me wrong. I appreciate his mother most of the time. But, I'd like him to 'cut the apron strings' and look to me, and even himself, for more of his answers."

Kerry rushed to his mother's defense.

"She just wants to help," he said. "I ask for help and she is willing to give it. What's wrong with that?"

"I'm not sure," I said. "Let's find out what's bothering Darla."

"I'll tell you what's bugging me," she said, looking over at Kerry. "I want you to stand on your own feet. I respect you a lot more when you solve your own problems. When you call your mom with every little thing that's bothering you, I lose respect for you. And she seems to call you when she has the slightest concern about you. All of that bugs me."

I was beginning to get the picture.

"Sounds like your mother enjoys her relationship with you, Kerry," I said. "And in many ways it sounds healthy. But, your wife wants to feel like number one in your life. Maybe it's time to push away from your mother a little more."

"What about my mother?" he said. "She's going to feel rejected. She's always been in my life and I know she still likes to talk to me."

"It's not like you have to reject her," I said. "You can still have a relationship, but not a triangle. There's not enough room in your marriage for three people."

Darla was obviously encouraged by my counsel.

"I believe in you Kerry," she said. "I'm proud of the way you handle problems. I want to see you handle more of them on your own, without input from her. If you need more encouragement, I want you to get it from me."

"Yeah, I can understand that," he said.

We talked more about how Kerry would set more boundaries on his mother's influence in their lives. We discussed ways he could let his mother know he appreciated her, but needed to develop his individuality, for the sake of himself as well as his marriage.

Encouraging, Educational, But Not Enabling

So here's the deal: In *Love and Logic* language, we encourage and support others to solve their own problems. We reflect that we know they are fully capable of figuring out life for themselves, and in doing so we empower them. We don't simply tell them it's their problem, but like in Jim's story about Nancy, we can throw out ideas about how others have worked on their problems. This sends a strong unstated message about their capabilities.

We also want to let others know that we too, can manage our own lives. At times we have to send that message quite loudly to those who would try to take care of us. We want to convey to everyone: *Life has it's challenges, but I've made it this far quite well, and I can continue my journey with your encouragement. I don't need anyone to take care of me.*

Now this message is not going to sit well with some people, especially Card-Carrying Codependents who believe their mission in life is to tell us how to live. These people are often well-intended, much like I was with my wife and many others are with me. They are, however, misguided, and it is our job to tell them so. (I heard that groan!)

Yes, it is our job to inform people how to treat us, and it is especially important to inform them how they can be Encouraging, and at times even Educational, but they cannot be Enabling. There is a big difference between these three. Let's look a bit closer, in reverse order.

What We Don't Need:

Enabling. We don't need anyone to solve our problems for us, as tempting as that might be at times. We don't need anyone enabling (reinforcing) our weaknesses. Having a mother nurse our wounds and beat up our bullies was fine when we were five, maybe even six or seven, but not so good when we were fifteen and beyond. We need to flex our own muscles. We need to peck our way out of our shells and discover we can manage life quite effectively, thank you, and by doing so we grow in self-esteem and self-respect.

So, even if I give you the message I can't make it on my own, don't believe it. I can. Even if I ask you to solve my problems, please don't do it. I'll figure it out. *My mistakes help me grow and not make bigger ones in the future.*

What to Do:

Educate: As I invite you into the sacred space of my problems, it is often helpful to share your stories with me. You can softly share how others have handled similar problems, without implying I handle them the same way. You can ask me if I'd like more information about how others have solved similar problems. But again, don't give me too much information. Don't overwhelm me with ways you've tackled problems in your life. There are only similarities in our problems—not identical issues.

Encouragement: The most powerful tool you can offer is encouragement—especially words that suggest "I can manage my own problems effectively." As you believe in me, I begin to believe in myself.

When one of my counselees faces a particularly challenging situation, I often offer the following words of encouragement:

> *You've faced similar problems in the past. How did that work for you?*
> *I know you have the strength and wisdom to face this challenge.*
> *You have many friends and resources to call upon to face this problem.*
> *You're a very bright individual with incredible wisdom to face this difficulty.*
> *I'm here to support you in anything you do.*

Can you see how this encouragement builds up rather than puts down? Can you see how this encouragement helps us reach within for our own answers? When we face and solve our own problems, we come out the other side stronger than ever. We develop self-confidence to face any struggle.

Dancing With Problems Together

Do you see how we can be in a relationship with another without being overly dependent on the other to solve our problems? This can be a very exciting dance.

My wife, Christie, and I dance through our problems together. I know she is working at developing her interior design business—

not at my pace or in my way. She faces problems differently than I do. She is more thoughtful and deliberate.

I, on the other hand, barrel ahead with my problems. I'm a bit more headstrong and reckless, which at times gets me into trouble. She encourages me to find my solutions and live with the consequences, both good and bad. I know I have her respect in caring for my life, and I give her respect in caring for her life. We practice healthy boundaries and gently remind each other when we slip into codependent caretaking.

How is this dance going for you? Are there relationships in your life that slip carelessly from encouragement to enabling? Are there people who would control you if you allowed it? These are boundaries needing reinforcement, *and I know you'll find a way to set those boundaries in place—even if it takes a mistake or two to get there*. The healthy dance is well worth it.

Run This Experiment

It's that time again—time to take what you've learned in this chapter and apply it to your life. We want you to consider how this information applies to your relationships and practice *encouraging others to solve their own problems, as well as encouraging others to allow you to solve your own problems*. Let's walk through five steps to help you learn this principle.

1. Consider one of your most pressing relationship problems.
2. Think about how are you dealing with it when it comes to *seeking encouragement* or *education*.
3. Have you allowed anyone to give you too much advice, enabling you **not** to face your own problems?
4. Think about how you lean on others, and how this makes you overly dependent.
5. Now, prepare to change. Make a plan for how you will seek encouragement, but **not** become overly dependent on others to solve your problems.

Facing your own problems will help you feel strong and secure. Setting limits on the advice others give you will teach them a valuable lesson as well—that you can solve many of your own problems.

Remember: Try it. Test it. Tweak it. This will be our pattern for the entire book. Nothing works perfectly each time, and some tools work more effectively for some than for others.

Now that you've got this tool under your belt, let's move forward to *creating strategic planning sessions*. We'll learn how to set up times for discussing your progress in relationships and ways to make these sessions a normal part of your relational life.

6

Creating Strategic Planning Sessions

"I just got lost in thought. It was unfamiliar territory."

—UNKNOWN

Fearing the Discussion We Really Need to Have

Steve had been worried about his friend, Jeff, and finally, over coffee, got up the nerve to talk with him.

"Jeff," he began, "I'm worried about you. Have you been sick? I noticed that you kept falling asleep on the drive to the lake last week. You're always so excited about our fishing trips and have a lot to say, but not during our last couple of trips."

"Ah, Steve. I swear that I haven't slept for the last six months. I might as well tell you what's going on.

You know about all the mistakes I made when I was young, the drugs, the alcohol. And I've been going though the Hepatitis C treatments and now I've got more problems."

"But you've been clean for years, Jeff." I protested. "That's not a problem now is it?"

"No, but my old life style has come back to haunt me. My last tests came back and the Doc says I'm HIV Positive."

"Oh, Jeff," Steve exclaimed, "I'm so sorry. That must be a terrible load to carry."

"Well, I can handle it myself, but this news is going to kill my dad."

"I know you're tight with your dad. But he's the kind of guy that can handle the news if you level with him. You've shared all about your past with him and he's been very supportive. You owe it to him to let him know about this. You just gotta tell him."

" I just can't do it. Telling him is going to be the hardest thing I've ever done. That's why I haven't been able to sleep. I agonize over it every night."

Steve Comes up with an Amazing Question

"Well Jeff. I know it's really going to be hard, but answer this. How *long* is it going to be hard for you?"

"What do you mean?"

"I mean literally, how long is it going to take to tell him, two minutes, three minutes, or what? You said it was going to be the hardest thing you've ever had to do, but is it going to be hard for the rest of you life, or for just a few minutes? You're tough. Can you handle something difficult for a couple of minutes?"

Jeff's eyes lit up for the first time in weeks, and he blurted out, "I never thought of it that way. All I've been able to think of is how hard it would be. I was so obsessed with that that I couldn't think of anything else. I guess I can handle anything for a few minutes. *Thanks!*"

The following day, Jeff came to Steve, looking like a new man. "Steve. I slept last night for the first time in months. Man, I feel better."

"Let me guess. You told your dad?"

"Yea, I did, and I couldn't believe how well he took the news. What a relief!"

How many times have we all found ourselves in the same predicament, needing to have a conversation with someone, putting it off and putting it off, thinking about how uncomfortable it would be? Then once it's over, we wondered why we wasted all our energy.

Worry is the price we pay in advance for
95 percent of the things that never happen.

From Worry to Mad to Aha!

"Can I talk to you?" my friend, Tom, asked seriously as I whisked by him in the hall of our office.

"Now?" I answered somewhat distracted.

"Well, when you've got time," he answered.

I took a moment to consider my plans. I had a client waiting in the waiting room, wanted to grab a quick cup of coffee, and needed to take a bathroom break before my session.

"How about in an hour," I said, without stopping.

"Sure," he said with that knowing look in his eye.

I went to the bathroom, grabbed my coffee and started my next session. I was a bit distracted by Tom's request to talk to me, wondering if he had good or bad news.

As soon as my session was over I rushed down the hall to Tom's office.

"What's up?" I asked.

"That's what I wanted to ask you," he said smiling. "You've been muttering about the cell phone company for the past three days. Seems like that's all you're talking about. Suing them. Getting your money back. Man, are you sure it's worth all that energy? Is this the direction you want for your life? Spending your energy in anger and not making a plan for correcting the problem?"

His questions caught me by surprise. I *thought* I was sure about all of it. I *thought* I was sure I was 'right.' I *thought* I was sure I wanted to sue them, and I was very sure I wanted my money back. Still, I know when Tom calls me aside on anything, there's usually at least a kernel of truth in what he's saying.

I sat and looked at Tom for a moment, wondering about what he was saying. Was I so wrapped up in this "mad" that I had forgotten about my friends, family and life goals? Was I so uptight about suing the phone company for three hundred dollars that I created tension in my office? What about my values of peace?

"I don't like how I've been treated, Tom," I said. "I want what is right!"

"Sure you do," he said. "And you're going to spend a lot of energy and focus to get it," he said in his professorial voice. "But, is it worth it—really? Do you think it's possible that you need to step back and look at your decision? Do you think all this energy you spend stewing could be better spent gathering information, talking to the phone company and seeing if you could work something out with them?"

Talking with Tom was helpful to me. I had been on a focused fast track, collecting information to use against the cellular phone company. I had all but ignored my staff, my health, my family and most important, myself. I wasn't practicing any of the *Love and Logic* tools I have talked about thus far in the book.

Tom reminded me that day of some things I had completely forgotten, and that is the tool for this chapter: *creating a strategic planning session*.

Strategic Planning Session

So, what is a *strategic planning session?* This may sound like an officious meeting of the CEO/CFO/AFL-CIO, or some other high and mighty board, but it's not. It's simply a time when you pull back from what you're doing and reconsider—much like what Tom did with me in the midst of my scurrying about. A strategic planning session is an opportunity to consider how you're going to handle various situations so that you don't go into them impulsively, ill-prepared and misfiring.

Remember that in everything we do, we're always mindful that some things work, and some things don't. We're not promising everything in this book is going to be magic, only that *some* things will be magic. It's your job to figure out which ones are magic and which ones must be discarded. In everything, we're mindful of the *Love and Logic* principle that *mistakes are great opportunities for learning*, with kids and adults of all ages.

And how do you do that? You guessed it—through the *strategic planning sessions* where you work through our formula: *try, trust, test, tweak, and test again.* Your strategic planning sessions will be the place where you consider what you've been doing with the significant people in your life to see if it's working. You're going to want answers to the following questions:

What are my goals for my relationships?
What have I been doing to reach my goals?
How have those strategies been working?
How should I tweak them so they work better?
What is the next thing to do?

Referring back to these questions throughout this book, and in your daily life with the people around you, will keep you on track. Keeping your goals in mind and remembering nothing works perfectly, keeps you moving forward and excited about your progress.

Let me show you how this worked for one couple recently.

Ted and Alice

I've been working with Ted and Alice for several months. Married for over twenty years, they've had plenty of time to discover what they like about each other as well as the things that drive each other crazy. They came to me to eliminate some things now threatening the stability of their marriage.

During the time we've worked together we've tried many things that worked, and a handful of things that didn't seem to mesh with their personalities. Ted, an engineer by profession, liked tools that were clear and direct. I suspected he would really like *creating a strategic planning session* where he and Alice reviewed their progress. He didn't like wasting any time in our sessions and wanted to make sure we had forward progress.

Alice was more carefree, willing to spend sessions talking about problems. More than anything, she wanted to be heard and understood by Ted, and was uncertain how to accomplish that.

"I want Ted to show more interest in my life," Alice said during a recent session. "I'm not sure how to make that happen."

"I'm willing to do that Alice," Ted said matter of factly. "You need to give me more feedback on how to do that, since I thought I already did it."

Alice looked at Ted and smiled.

"You certainly talk to me and I appreciate that," she said. "You ask me about my day, and that feels good to me. You empathize with me when I'm struggling with something."

"But . . ." he said, leaning toward her. "Something's missing, obviously. What am I missing here?"

"Great job," I said to Ted. "I think you're about to get some more information."

"This may be asking too much of you, Ted," she said, "but I'd like you to anticipate what's happening in my day and ask specific questions about that."

"Okay," he said slowly, considering what she had just asked for. "You want me to ask more specific questions about your day?"

"Yes," Alice said. "And I'd like you to remember what I have going in my day so you can show interest in it."

I watched and listened as Ted and Alice communicated very effectively. They were using tools we have already discussed in this book, such as *neutralizing arguments* and *practicing empathy*. They needed little involvement from me.

"I think I can do that Alice," he said, smiling. "I'm going to do my best. But, how will I know how I'm doing?"

"I'll let you know," she said, reaching out for his hand. "I appreciate your hard work in this marriage. This will mean a lot to me."

"Folks," I said, "I haven't had to do much as I've listened to you. Pat yourselves on the back for work nicely done. I do have one more tool for you to put in your tool box."

"What's that?" Ted asked.

"It's called *creating a strategic planning session*. This means you will sit down in a week or so and reflect upon how you've been doing with what Alice asked you to do."

"We call those *Feedback Circles* at work," Ted said. "We sit down every week to review our goals and objectives to see if we're on target. Is that what you mean?"

"Pretty much," I said. "Nothing works perfectly, and we need to expect things may need to be modified, tweaked and tried again."

"Sounds good to me," Alice said, while Ted nodded his approval.

"Okay then," I said. "Let's meet next week for our *strategic planning session*, otherwise known as counseling, to see how you've done at listening to Alice and practicing your own *strategic planning session*."

In The Office

You've read about how I got so caught up in my emotion, and what I impulsively thought was "right and wrong," that I wasn't able to step back and accurately measure whether what I was doing was working. Then we looked at how Ted and Alice eagerly used the *Love and Logic* principles to work through problems effectively in their relationship. Now, let's look at another scenario.

The office-mates; that place where many of us spend a good portion of our lives.

We spend a large percentage of our lives on the job, and often work closely with people we wouldn't normally choose to spend so much time with.

Our friend, Sharon, works in a medical office where three women co-share responsibilities. Sharon told me recently she asked the other two women to meet with her to discuss what they could do to share responsibilities effectively.

Previous to this meeting, someone was always blaming the others for work not getting done. Feelings were always getting hurt, tensions were high and productivity was impacted.

Sharon sat down with her workmates in a strategic planning session to discuss the problem. They agreed about the importance of getting along, and the incredible cost to each of them personally and professionally to continue fault-finding. They agreed rather than to focus on what they were doing "wrong," to build upon each other's strengths and reinforce the gains from working as a team.

When I asked Sharon recently how things were going at work, she told me, "I can't believe the difference the meeting had on our relationship. We created clear boundaries for who was going to do what, and agreed to never gossip about the others or blame anyone for something that didn't get done. It is so much nicer to go to work."

"So everything has been ironed out?" I asked.

"Well, not quite," she said smiling. "We're not perfect, but things are **way** better."

Using High Tech Communications Wisely

I think this is the perfect spot to insert a quick word on high tech communications. It fits in perfectly with strategic planning. Knowing what you are going to send out into cyberspace before you hit the send button takes planning.

I understand not long ago, the Blackberry world was rocked when their email system went down for 24 hours. People weren't sure how to react. All of a sudden they were reduced to the old ways of doing things—speaking in person (yikes!) or on the phone (double yikes!).

Now I fully realize in this day and age we are used to instant communication. We want to instant message, email or text. Who doesn't love that little "ding" or "buzz" that happens when our cell phone signals someone is thinking about us?

In our world of Love and Logic Magic for Lasting Relationships, however, where we want to enhance ways to get along, there are dangers associated with this high tech world we live in. Consider the following example of an email I received recently, wrongly sent to me and intended for someone else.

Hey Jim. Cant make it to ur party tonite, but glad not to b there anyway since Cathy will b there. Always hated her. She is so full of herself. No air left in the room after she uses it all. O well. Maybe next time. Jack.

Now, understand Jack sent this email to me, not Jim. Then, imagine I have some idea as to who Cathy is. Additionally, consider who else might have received this email. Finally, consider this email is forever saved on my hard drive.

Yes, email is a fast and often effective means of communication. However, many people use email too casually, sending messages off in the wrong direction, saying things they later regret, with (perceived) meaning by the receiver that the sender cannot control. Slow down. Think through what you want to say and how you want to say it. You'll be thankful when you catch yourself reaching for the "send" button in time to give your message a second thought.

The Mistake Mindset

Everybody makes mistakes! It's what you do with them, and ways you think about them, that makes all the difference in the world. Remember, according to *Love and Logic* principles, the main thing to keep in mind is: *mistakes are learning situations.* Use them wisely. Your *strategic planning sessions* are great times and places to review how you're doing with your new tools.

With that in mind, here are some additional ideas to help you take yourself and your mistakes a little less seriously. We call it *the mistake mindset.*

One, *use small mistakes to stop you from making larger ones.* This first step is possibly the most important to understand. When we realize every mistake is an opportunity not to make a larger one, we can embrace it. When we 'lean in' to these mistakes, seeking the larger truths inherent in every one, we stop being angry with ourselves for making them in the first place.

A recent speeding ticket (yes, another one!!) was enough to grab my attention again, reminding me of my propensity to push the gas pedal more than needed. It was only a hundred dollar error, way enough to get my mind back in the driving game, slowing me down and alerting me to my driving. Rather than curse the ticket, I was able to think of it as a wake up call.

Two, *discover what can be learned from your mistakes*. Since every mistake is an opportunity not to make a larger mistake, the trick is to figure out what lesson you're supposed to learn. What larger mistake might you avoid by making the small ones you're working on today?

Using my speeding ticket again as an example, the ticket not only warned me of larger tickets and consequences I would receive if I didn't pay closer attention, but the deeper value of adhering to laws of the road that are there for everyone's benefit.

Three, *use your strategic planning sessions to review your mistakes and ways to avoid larger ones in the future*. Since you will make mistakes, you will need to set aside times to review and critique them. You'll need time to reflect upon your mistakes and understand how you will change your life so as to not make the same mistakes, or larger ones, in the future.

Learning occurs when we obtain new information and then integrate it into our lives. Getting a speeding ticket wouldn't change my behavior unless I reflected upon it, anticipated how a larger ticket might affect me, as well as attached this event to deeper values and meaning in my life. A *mini-strategic planning session* allowed me to consider these issues and change my behavior from the inside out—rather than from the outside in. (The cost of the ticket versus adhering to deeply held values.)

Four, *always build upon strengths*. Even in making your mistakes, recognize you've already avoided larger ones. Practice keeping mistakes in perspective, giving yourself credit for not making larger mistakes now. Consider what you're doing right and pat yourself on the back.

By considering your deeply held values you not only enhance your self-esteem (by affirming who you really want to be and moving toward that person), but move your behavior in that direction. Consider your strengths and affirm them.

Five, *reinforce positive gains*. Sitting in your office, congratulate each other on the things you're doing right. Notice and applaud ways you've avoided larger mistakes. Notice the gains you're making from your current mistakes. Again, practice keeping things in perspective. Things could be worse.

How have you done at neutralizing arguments? Give yourself a pat on the back for those gains. Have you learned how to set enforceable consequences at times? Notice those gains. Are you practicing these tools, finding the ones that work best for you? Good job.

Six, *no mistakes are fatal*. When we understand we're going to make mistakes creating growth opportunities, we take them a bit less seriously. People who view mistakes as fatal are boring, serious and a touch dangerous. We don't want to be around that mentality. We consider mistakes as a necessary part of our learning.

Finally, *have fun*. Making mistakes *is not* serious business. We all make mistakes. Those using *Love and Logic* principles to guide their lives face their mistakes and use them to avoid making larger mistakes. They use strategic planning sessions to organize their thoughts, making plans for improving their lives according to the mistakes they've already made.

Analyzing Mistakes

Armed with a healthy *mistake mindset,* you're ready to sit down during a *strategic planning session* to determine what you've done wrong and what you'll do to not repeat mistakes, to not make larger mistakes, and to tweak your life so as to make your relationships healthier and happier.

This requires having what we call *the third eye*. We're not talking about some Cyclopsian oddity, but rather the ability to step outside of yourself long enough to take an objective appraisal of your situation. In order to really follow the recipe of *try, trust, test, tweak and test again* you must have an eye that steps outside your current situation, emotions and all, to "see" what is really going on.

While this may sound easy enough, it is really quite tricky. You see, when you're in the middle of the muddle of relating, emotions get stirred up. The almighty Ego gets involved and issues like "being right" get set in motion. Defenses get activated and we struggle against having to admit we've made a mistake. No problem. We've got the answers for you.

The answer comes from rehearsing *the mistake mindset*. We're not in trouble. We haven't done anything wrong. We're safe. With our *third eye*, we step outside our situation (called detaching), settle into our *strategic planning session* with our mate, and consider what's going on. We review our recipe analyzing mistakes:

What are my goals for my relationships?
What have I been doing to reach my goals?
How have those strategies been working?
How should I tweak them so they work better?
What is the next thing to do?

Your life is rich with information. All you have to do is sit back, reflect upon this information, and then make new decisions based on what you've learned. You must use that bit of Einstein in you to consider what you're doing, why it's not working the way you'd like, and what you can do to make it work better. It's all fairly simple.

Creating and Embracing Change

While understanding what *needs* to be changed is fairly simple, enacting that change is a bit more complicated. Why? Because, for as much as we want change, we also resist it. We've spent a lot of time creating a world just the way we like it—or so we think. Deconstructing our world can be tricky business. Let's consider some implications of change.

Change requires us to upset the apple cart. I don't know about you, but I cling tenaciously to my life, just the way I've constructed it. Additionally, others cling to their lives just as tenaciously. I learned about this first hand recently.

Two weeks ago I received an unexpected visit from my neighbors in the office condominium complex where I have my office. The business neighbor asked if he could purchase my office condo. I hadn't considered selling, but having someone make an offer on the spot was inviting. I told him I would think about his offer and get back to him in a few days.

During the next several days I was surprised by the array of emotions I felt. While I was excited with the offer at first, I then felt anxiety. What would I do for an office if I sold this one? How would my staff react to this possibility? Would relationships be strained in the process? Even before accepting their offer I felt anticipatory anxiety and apprehension. These thoughts and emotions swirled about in my mind in unending motion during the next few days.

Discussing the offer with my wife, we decided the opportunity was worth pursuing. I decided to present the idea to my staff, fully expecting some apprehension, but overall support. Wrong!

Gathering my staff, I announced the serendipitous offer from our neighbors. I shared my excitement with them about creating a new office somewhere else in town. I shared the apprehension I first felt, but the shift of certainty I now felt. I waited for their enthusiastic support.

And waited . . .

And waited . . .

Not only were they not enthusiastically supportive, but they voiced criticism after criticism. They voiced concerns, counterarguments, and disapproval for the idea. They thought moving was a huge mistake.

I had forgotten an invaluable lesson regarding change: *people usually resist change because of the chaos it initially creates.* Of course they would resist this change. Why wouldn't they? It was going to upset their apple cart, and they needed time to process the situation.

It has been two weeks since that difficult meeting, and I'm pleased to say the staff is processing their feelings, embracing the challenges, and preparing for a possible move. We're still in the middle of the chaos, but we're working together as a team to make this opportunity work for us.

Making Your Relationships Work

We are all in the process of change—for the better. You're reading this book because you want to learn new ways of getting along. You want your relationships to be healthier, happier and more reward-ing. To do so you must *create and embrace change*. Your *strategic planning session* will be the forum for you to evaluate what you're doing, how well it's working, and what needs to be changed.

Unfortunately, most of us are practicing strategies that simply don't work. We keep doing them because we're creatures of habit. In fact, we now know the brain likes similarities and patterns, and unless we hit a speed bump (mistakes with consequences) we might go on doing something forever.

There's one last "boat rocking" point to make before we end the chapter—*something needs to be changed*. Since we're all mortal, and make mistakes, we must embrace receptivity to change. Let's face it—our mate wants something more from us, our friends want something more from us, and how about the boss? Plus, we want something more from them. We want to have healthier conflict. We want greater intimacy. We want more affection and greater understanding. We want *change*.

Are you ready? Change does not happen without initiative, effort and discomfort. Just as I had to face uncertainty in moving my office and upsetting my staff, you must also face the discomfort that comes from facing change. Just as Ted had to learn to listen in new ways to his wife, Alice, you must also look and listen in new ways to what your friends and family want from you.

Now, here's the exciting part. After initial discomfort and even chaos, comes *The New Normal*. Old ways of relating slip into the past and new patterns of interacting take center stage. There are better ways of interacting, and you will learn these as you *create strategic planning sessions* where you analyze and embrace mistakes. This process always leads to relationship growth.

Run This Experiment

You're more than halfway through the book and know what to expect at this point. It's your turn to practice. It's your turn to take what you've learned in this chapter and give it a test drive. You've got to see if this buggy has the wheels you need.

So, consider where you are with your primary relationships. Choose one relational situation. Maybe you'll choose your marriage. Perhaps you'll choose a situation with your co-worker or even a parent. Ask the following questions:

1. What is happening? How do you feel about the relationship?
2. Step back and reflect upon the situation with your third eye, in a detached way.
3. Consider creating a strategic planning session where you discuss how the relationship is going? Know what you want and be prepared to ask for change.
4. Contact the person and have the meeting. Take in as much information as you can and use it to enhance and improve the relationship.
5. Enjoy!

Remember: Try it. Test it. Tweak it. We use smaller problems to avoid bigger ones. We use our planning sessions to brainstorm ideas for change. It's all good.

In this next chapter you'll discover you're not alone in this growth process, and we'll explore an incredibly powerful tool: *sharing the load*.

7

Sharing the Load

"We may have all come on different ships, but we're in the same boat now."
—MARTIN LUTHER KING, JR.

"Hang on," my buddy yelled in my ear. His scream scared me nearly as much as the sight ahead. Twenty yards just off to our left, the waves of another river poured into the one we were rafting down.

"Steer to the right," the guide screamed. "Everybody get a hold. Work together. Here we go!"

Just then I felt the raft buckle as the waves crashed against the left side of the raft. Our screams were filled with a mixture of terror, delight and pure adrenaline.

We swept through the rapids too quickly to feel the full extent of the fear we would feel moments later. There was no time to think; only to hold on.

Passing through the sudden jolt of powerful current, sensing the raft bend to the surge of water, only heightened our excitement. "Controlled danger," our guide had explained, "would lead to an incredible thrill. Everyone doing their part will keep us safe."

He was right, and that is what this chapter is about: *sharing the load of solving problems*.

I was reminded of this principle during the particularly difficult last year in my mother's life. With my ninety-year-old mother failing in health, I watched my two sisters and sister-in-law work seamlessly together, ensuring the continuity of her care, maintaining her dignity, and simply getting along.

While providing care to my mother always appeared seamless, during a recent visit my sister shared the following.

"David," she said thoughtfully, "caring for mom this last year has been the most difficult thing I've ever done. It was exhausting at times. Being from a family of powerful women, we found ourselves stepping on each other's toes when this all started. We had to learn to work together. We sat down all the time and shared feelings, making sure no one felt overburdened with the responsibilities. We recognized our personal limitations and tried to give grace to each other when we were less than sensitive to each other."

"Sounds tiring," I said. "I couldn't do what you all have done."

"There was a need," she said tearfully, "and we all wanted to do it. I wouldn't take any of it back, and now that Mom's gone we are all closer because of it. We had to keep reminding ourselves of the importance of sharing the load and solving problems together."

Working with another couple, I had the perfect opportunity to introduce this tool. I listened as they shared their history of how they had gotten together.

Daniel came from a working class family just outside Pittsburgh. His father worked in the steel industry, as had his grandfather. Through hard work, his parents had scraped and saved for him to attend college, the first in his family to do so, and the only sibling to attain a degree. Daniel never lost sight of this small-town, hard-working heritage, and always dreamed of going back to a small town to raise a family.

Deborah, on the other hand, was raised in the heart of Seattle. Both parents were prominent attorneys who worked hard, were active in politics, theater and the symphony. She attended private schools and went to an Ivy League university.

Daniel and Deborah's strikingly different worlds collided in a small coffee shop in Seattle where they struck up an exciting conversation. Their differences attracted them to each other, as well as creating an interesting and exciting tension.

As is often the case, their differences formed the basis for a dynamic friendship, but they also held the potential for conflict. You'll see what I mean shortly.

Daniel decided early to leave the blue-collar environment of small-town Pennsylvania and find a better living in the suburbs of Seattle. Deborah had no plans to leave Seattle, except for possibly moving to an even larger city like Los Angeles or New York. Can you sense a power struggle brewing? Although they both came from dramatically disparate backgrounds, they had something very important in common—stubborn resolution. This would be the foundation for both their success and their undoing.

Their friendship blossomed quickly, and before either had a chance to consider long-term ramifications, they were married. Deborah assumed they would remain in Seattle where she would attend law school, while Daniel assumed she would work in city planning in a suburb. He would continue teaching school in one of the smaller communities.

The Power Struggle

Given that two people often come from different locales, with different family upbringings, and sometimes even dramatically different cultures, it is a wonder that anybody gets along. Think about it. Consider the magnitude of the gulf that must be crossed in order to find our way to each other.

Now add another significant factor. *We often enter relationships thinking our way of doing things is 'the right way,' and expect others to conform to our manner of living.*

"Why does she do things the way she does?" Daniel asked, almost rhetorically. "I just don't get her."

"I could say the same thing about you," Deborah said. "Why do

I have to conform to your way of doing things?"

"Where are you two stuck?" I asked, after having gathered information about their background, meeting and marriage.

"He wants to move outside the city and I'm an urban dweller," Deborah said. "It's that simple, and yet we can't seem to move past it."

"I've always imagined raising our kids in a smaller country town, like the one I was raised in," Daniel said. "We can move an hour away and still be close enough to the city to suit both of us."

"Not for me," Deborah said quickly. "You know I want to go back to school, and it's not going to be easy living an hour from Seattle."

"An hour is doable," Daniel said. "I think we can make it work."

Deborah looked at me for help, clearly unhappy with the options Daniel was proposing.

"I don't want to live an hour from the city!" she said again, this time raising her voice for emphasis. "In fact, I'm not going to live an hour from the city."

"I don't get it," Daniel said. "I can't stand the noises of the city, and don't want our kids schooled in an inner city school. You know how I feel about that."

"Hey folks," I said. "You don't seem to be getting anywhere with this. I'd like to introduce a principle I think will transform how you talk to each other. I think practicing this principle could really unlock this power struggle you seem caught in."

Both turned to me in anticipation. The pressure was now on me to deliver on my promise. I hoped this would be one of the *Love and Logic* tools they would find empowering.

"What if there was a way to work together, discovering a 'win/win' solution? What if you really believed both of you were 'right' in different ways? If you really, really believed that, there'd be no reason to argue—right?"

"Sounds interesting," Daniel said, with Deborah nodding.

Early in the book I relayed the powerful truth that is central to the work of *Love and Logic Institute*—*We share control over how we're going to solve problems.* I could see how this truth would help Daniel and Deborah eliminate conflict and lead them into cooperative living. This principle forms the backbone for the tool we're sharing in this chapter: healthy relationship are built upon the principle of *sharing the load*.

Blame

I let my questions sink in, considering how to move them along in their relationship. I decided to keep Daniel and Deborah waiting a bit longer while I highlighted what they were doing, exploring how it was or wasn't working for them.

"As I watch you," I said, "you seem stuck. You seem to want to blame the other for their point of view. You seem to want to coerce your mate into thinking the way you think."

Both watched me and listened carefully.

"Is it right to live in the city or the suburbs?" I asked.

Both seemed surprised by my question.

"Well," Daniel began, "I suppose that depends on each person's preference. I prefer to live in the suburbs, so that's the right answer for me."

"And I prefer the city," Deborah said smiling, "so that's the right answer for me."

"Exactly," I said. "But I'm not sure either of you answered my question. Is it right to live in the city or the suburbs?"

"No," they answered in unison.

"I agree," I said, smiling. "Of course, neither place is *right*. It's all a matter of preference. Problems occur in relationships when we become too welded to our position. We find fault, affix blame. We are so often tempted to think we've got the superior position, when really each of us has, and is entitled to, our own point of view."

I paused for a moment.

"So this conversation isn't really about city or suburb living, but whether you two can create enough room in your relationship for differing points of view. I believe you can. But, in order to do so you will have to take a deep breath, be considerate of the other and his/her point of view, and let go of any desire to 'win.' You will have to do what I call *share the load*."

Now I was ready to share our next invaluable lesson.

Sharing the Load Through Cooperation

Perhaps the greatest area where couples get stuck is getting locked in deciding who owns the problem, and most important, who's going to solve it. In fact, most couples aren't even aware that there are other options besides getting locked in power struggles over problems. That's what makes this tool so powerful. Couples can share, and we believe *should* share, in owning and solving problems. Let's zero in on each of these ideas and see how they not only apply to Daniel and Deborah, but to your life as well.

Sharing the Load of Responsibility for the Problem. Imagine how delighted you would feel if someone came to you and said, "I know we have a tough problem to overcome. I know I play a part in this problem and want you to know I acknowledge that."

I don't know about you, but if Christie (my wife) came to me in the middle of a complicated issue and said those words, I'd reach over and kiss her. Why? Because by saying she co-owns the problem she is reassuring me of several things:

- That she acknowledges this isn't all about me and something I've done wrong;
- That she is willing to look at her part in the problem;
- That she is more than likely willing to move ahead in solving the problem together.

This is big stuff! *It's not all my fault.* This is the exact location where people get stuck—blaming one another for what's going wrong. If no one is wrong, and we've only got to focus on solving the problem, we're halfway home. Can you see the power in this principle?

Blame is a particularly damaging tactic many use, thinking they are somehow solving the problem. After all, if I can make the problem belong to someone else, it's no longer on my plate. I'm exonerated, free, able to sit back and watch someone else manage the problem.

But of course it doesn't work this way. The one blamed never sits well with this, nor should they. Blame is a narrow, rigid definition of 'right and wrong,' as opposed to the broader, larger perspective that *we are in this together*. Blame isolates, divides and shames.

Sharing the load of responsibility for the problem never blames, shames or isolates. Sharing the load brings us together. We become a team, working on something outside ourselves—the problem.

How will this work for Daniel and Deborah? If they agree to *share the load of responsibility for the problem*, they will stop blaming each other for their dilemma. They will affirm the unique traits they each brought to the relationship, and acknowledge how those unique traits, (one being an urbanite, the other a small city guy) are qualities that can enhance their relationship. Neither is wrong for what they want. Neither is bad. These same unique traits that drew them together have created a problem, but, no worries. Problems can always be solved.

Unfortunately there are times when we are so personally invested in a problem it's impossible to see our own piece of the blame. This is called *being human*. But, have you ever noticed how much easier it is to know what others ought to do to solve their problems. How many times have we been stumped about how to deal with our own children, while at the same time knowing exactly what the neighbors ought to do about their kids? That brings us to another solution to the problem of blame.

Sharing the Load of Responsibility for the Solution

The second tower of power revolutionizing your relationships is *sharing the load of responsibility for the solution*. When we stop blaming each other and co-own the problem, it only follows that we will move together to figure out a solution.

Notice that I use the word *responsibility*. This means it is not an option to opt out of this responsibility. You cannot look at your boss and say, "I don't want to solve this one. You take it." That would be ridiculous. You must stand up, step in and face the issue.

Upon inheriting her Aunt's house and some vacant land, Jennifer called her friend, Dale, a successful builder, with an offer of a partnership. She would provide the land and he would construct the homes. They would split the profits, but there was one condition. They would choose a different realtor from the one Dale used. Jennifer had never had a good feeling about Dale's realtor, and had wondered if he was taking advantage of Dale by selling below market value, or pulling other shading deals along the way.

Dale agreed to the condition, and the partnership was arranged. They chose a realtor Jennifer knew. All went well until both of them discovered the new realtor was lazy and the homes were languishing on the market. They were losing money by the day as the interest on the building loans ate up all the projected profits.

Their healthy relationship was turning sour. Each blamed the other. Dale blamed Jennifer for insisting on the different realtor. Jennifer's position was that Dale was to blame for not doing his due diligence. And they both blamed the realtor for locking them into a contract that they couldn't get out of. There was plenty of blame to go around. There just weren't any solutions, and a law suit was on the horizon.

Out of desperation, Dale and Jennifer hired a consultant to mediate the problem. This wise mediator knew they had to remove the personalities and the blame before they could make any headway.

"I'm wondering if it might be a good time to turn this into a game instead of a potential war," the mediator offered.

"It's no time for game playing," shouted Jennifer. "Dale just won't quit blaming me for bringing in the new realtor. He signed off on the contract. It's as much his fault as it is mine."

"I was doing fine with my business before Jennifer demanded that we change realtors. Now we're stuck with someone who isn't getting these houses sold and we are bleeding money, waiting for the contract to end. The realtor is holding us hostage. I don't know if I'm madder at her," he said pointing to Jennifer, "or the realtor!"

Let's Pretend

After hearing both Dale and Jennifer, the mediator said, "Let's play the pretend game. Let's pretend that this is not your problem, but is something happening to someone else.

"If I were to come to you to mediate a similar dispute with people from another company what would you tell those people?"

"I don't know what I'd tell them," Dale answered. Jennifer concurred.

"Well, if you did know what to tell them what would you say? Humor me and pretend that you do know."

"We'd have to tell them to forget about placing blame and focus on a solution."

"And what if they asked for some ideas?"

"Well," suggested Jennifer, "One suggestion I'd make is for them to consider buying their way out of the realtor's contract at a reduced cost, get a new broker, and move on. They could cut their losses that way."

"Have the two of you discussed that possibility?

"No." added Dale. "I guess we got so deep into the forest that we couldn't see the trees. This has been so upsetting to us. It's so much easier to see when it involves someone else."

"I guess I can see why you wanted us to pretend that the problem was not ours."

Facing the issues together is freeing. I don't know about you, but Christie and I have a very different tone and gentleness to our relating when we acknowledge, "We're in this together. We must find a solution to this problem."

Shifting from blame to mutual acceptance of responsibility made a huge difference in Jennifer and Dale's relationship. Changing their approach abruptly ended their power struggle, leading to a more open attitude where they shared the load of responsibility for the problem and the solution, making the difference between anger or friendship/tension or cooperation. They chose the latter.

Now let's explore how Daniel and Deborah used this principle to eliminate their power struggle.

Working with Daniel and Deborah to stop blaming each other, co-own the problem, and move into brainstorming new solutions made all the difference in the world. Instead of attacking each other's point of view, they moved into the ease of working as a team on a problem.

"I suppose we could live just outside the city," Deborah offered after making the mind-shift. "It's an easy commute to Seattle from Lynnwood or Kirkland."

Daniel then jumped in with some solutions of his own. "I guess I could see us living in one of the small districts in Seattle," he said. "I've always loved the Fremont district, and that's close to the University of Washington. It would be fun to raise a family near the water."

"Owning the problem as well as the solution seems to have freed you up to consider more options. How does this new attitude feel?" I asked them.

"Kind of crazy," Daniel added. "When I was set in my ways, thinking Deborah had to see my point of view and agree with it, we were both stuck. When we loosened up and shared the load, everything got easier."

Daniel and Deborah came only a few more times, finding they could move through any problem as long as they owned it together. Working together on the solution stopped them from blaming each other, working together on a situation, evokes the creative potential in all of us to find solutions.

The Cooperation Mindset

Where did we go wrong? When did we shift from holding hands when crossing the street to everyone looking out for themselves? It's a terrible shift, if you ask me, and this book is about moving back to a simpler, more graceful manner of living where we cooperate with each other to get where we want to go.

Remember, this book contains magic—*Love and Logic Magic for Lasting Relationships*. If you will employ these principles we firmly believe getting along is not only possible, but preferable.

Sharing the load is possible when we have a *cooperative mindset*. Consider these benefits of a cooperative mindset:

- Working together makes every task easier, every problem lighter, and solutions flow from our cooperative spirit.

- Working together creates harmony. Working individually creates disharmony, conflict and tension.
- Working together creates community. When we're "all in this together" we feel connected and solve problems faster, easier and with a sense of joy.
- Working together enhances self-esteem. We have a feeling of "belongingness," making us feel we are part of something greater than ourselves.
- Working together breeds teamwork, a skill necessary to many other aspects of life.

Can you see the value of working together? Can you imagine your world filled with cooperating with others, sharing the load of responsibility for the creation of problems as well as for finding solutions?

A Sense of Connection

Sharing the load has another magical impact on our wellbeing: we feel a powerful connection to each other. Studies have shown that we live longer, happier lives when we are connected to, and feel supported by each other.

While many of us complain loudly about our relationships, moaning about the impossibility of getting along with so and so, leave us alone in a cabin for two days and we're ready to talk to the walls. We simply crave human attention, affection and support.

A movie titled *The Story of Us*, made several years ago starring Bruce Willis and Michelle Pfeiffer, told the story of a couple who couldn't seem to get along. Bickering furiously at times, they separated repeatedly in order to end the battle. Each time, however, they realized how much they still cared about each other, and how dependent they were on feeling connected to someone who knew their history.

Not only did the characters in this drama care about each other, but they fulfilled a critical role—that of helping each other cope with the struggles of life. While they thought being alone would end their difficulties, they found themselves faced with a new set of problems associated with being alone and disconnected.

The movie ends on a hopeful note, suggesting they will find a way to cooperate with each other to end their emotional battles and achieve the intimacy both are seeking. Their story is our story, and their hope is our hope. We can cooperate with each other to share the load.

Synergy

No conversation on cooperation and *sharing the load* is complete without talking about *synergy*. Besides simply liking the sound of this word—it even sounds exciting—sharing any load does more than disperse the responsibility of a problem off one person's shoulders. There is much more that happens. It's called *synergy—the idea that the value of the group is greater than simply the sum of the individuals*. Something bigger is happening when two or more of us come together.

I must admit that I'm a synergy fanatic. While I work well as an individual, I absolutely love what happens when three or four people come together to brainstorm an idea. Why is that?

Because, I am locked in my own point of view. I can never not be "the guy who was raised in northwest Washington State, who has lived the majority of his life in Washington State, who went to schools in Washington State and now writes and practices as a psychologist in Washington State."

Now don't get me wrong. I'm not at all opposed to Washington State. In fact, I love it here. But, there is something enlivening when I sit in a coffee shop in upstate New York, downtown Manhatten or Todos Santos, Mexico, and listen to the conversation. I appreciate how each person faces a problem or a solution, from a different point of view. I love the new ideas others bring to the table.

In this same manner, I'm thrilled when people move from being locked in a power struggle over "who is right," and move into "how can we solve this problem together." I notice the palpable, definable, recognizable shift occur when they decide to stop fighting and start dreaming about solutions.

People are always surprised when this shift happens. Locked for so long in their myopic worlds, they are amazed when a kaleido-scope of possibilities emerges.

"What is this new world of possibilities?" they ask.

"It is not a new world at all," I think to myself, but I share, "It is simply opening our eyes to what was always there. We have some-thing of tremendous value to share with each other. Together we are so more than we are as individuals."

This is the power of *sharing the load*.

Run This Experiment

Are you feeling excited? While not every tool generates the same level of excitement for each person, *sharing the load*—seeing prob-lems and solutions in a new light—holds loads of potential for you.

Now it's your turn to practice.

Sit back and imagine:

How have you been blaming someone else for a particular problem?
What is your part in this problem?
How might you redefine the problem so that it's no one's fault?
What are some possible solutions to the problem?
Now sit down with this person and brainstorm possibilities.

Remember: Try it. Test it. Tweak it. And try it again. In the next chapter you'll discover another powerful tool for lessening conflict and creating harmony: *offering choices within limits*.

8

Offering Choices Within Limits

"There are two primary choices in life: to accept conditions as they exist, or accept the responsibility for changing them."

—DENIS WAITLEY

I'm always surprised at the simplicity of the *Love and Logic* approach and how effective it is. Not only is it one of the fastest growing parenting programs in the country, but now we've taken these same principles and applied them to adult relationships. The *Love and Logic* approach is, as we've said again and again, simple and logical. Practicing these tools will help you feel competent and encouraged in every relationship.

There are so many ways these principles and tools apply to our daily lives. A recent phone call reminded me of the next powerful tool in our collection: *offering choices within limits*.

"I can't stand living this way," the woman on the phone complained.

"What's going on?" I asked.

"I'm in love with a man who won't commit to our relationship," she said sadly. "We share so much in common and love each other deeply, but he can't commit."

"Won't commit," I said, correcting her.

"Yeah, that's right," she said. "He has his cake and is eating it too."

I was glad we were on the phone so she could not see me smile at her remark.

"Are you setting clear boundaries for him?" I asked.

"I hate to threaten anyone," she said. "So, no I'm probably not being as clear as I should be. I keep hoping he'll see how good our relationship is and make the decision to fully commit."

"And how is that working for you?" I asked.

"Terrible," she said, beginning to cry. "My life is a mess. I wait for the day when he'll decide to really commit to me, but this has been going on for three years and I see no change in sight. I get my hopes up and then they're dashed. I dream about being with him and then wait for the phone to ring. It's terrible."

"I doubt there will be any change until you are very clear, and you offer him choices within limits."

"I don't know what that means," she said. "Can you help me with that?"

"Yes, I can!," I said confidently. I knew some tools that might just help solve her problems.

After just a few minutes on the phone it became clear this woman, Ariana, whom I had never personally met, struggled with something that's difficult for most of us, and is our next powerful tool: *offering choices within limits*—offering choices, within limits, about how others can interact with you. The choices you offer are driven by what you need to feel safe and secure.

Each of us must decide, ahead of time, exactly what we need to feel safe, secure and effective. We need to rehearse, and be clear about how we expect to be treated, and what we will do if we're not treated that way. When I know what I need, and feel certain that I have options if I'm not treated that way, then I feel in control of my life. This is the *Love and Logic* way. Me controlling my world and allowing you to control yours.

Both you and Ariana must become aware of the environment, emotionally and physically, that you need in order to grow. You must tend to your life as if it were a garden, needing certain nutrients in order to blossom. You protect your Self, nurture your Self, and ensure that others respect your Self so you can grow. While others are never forced to respect your Self, you determine *the choices they have, within limits, if they want to interact with you.*

Let's look at how this works with a couple of ex-spouses.

Scott thought he had found the woman of his dreams. But after three years and a child, his marriage turned into a nightmare. Even though the split was ugly, Scott was determined to stay on the best terms possible with his ex-wife.

During visits and swaps when she was rude or short with him, he stayed focused on his goal to remain a good role model for their daughter. He kept smiling and noticing positives whenever he could. He listened with empathy and genuine concern when his ex vented.

Over time, the ex, Judy, couldn't help but appreciate Scott and his commitment to do the very best for their daughter. Judy found herself less tense when she was around him. Ultimately, she found she had to really work at staying bitter and resentful. Try as she might, she just couldn't fight with him like she used to.

Ex-spouses and former significant others can pose tricky, ongoing challenges, especially when there are kids and *new* spouses/ significant others involved.

If we really want to make it hard on ourselves, we can choose to focus on the things we cannot control and put lots of energy into those 'uncontrollables.' Happier people, however, seem to find ways to focus on things they **can** control.

Certainly, we cannot control our ex's behavior, our ex's new partner, our ex's new partner's behavior (unless it is inappropriate enough to take legal action). There are plenty of things we cannot control in situations such as these.

Fortunately, like Scott, we *can* control things like: How we communicate, how pleasant we keep our voices and most importantly, we can control our primary focus: doing the best we can to raise kids who are wonderful human beings.

Parents and step-parents who like their hair less gray and their blood pressure lower decide to figure out the things they can control and set limits using those controls. They make *enforceable* statements such as "I discuss the kids when I feel like I am being heard." or "We drive kids to practice when they wear seatbelts" or even "We'll be happy to pick up Sally from your house *after* 3 pm."

When discussions do take place, we can also choose whether we defend our positions to the death, or listen and do our very best to hear and understand the other person. We can focus on common interests and especially common goals (hopefully, the goal to do the best things for our kids). We can choose to be as civil and empathetic as possible in all our interactions.

We can also decide **not** to escalate tension or ill will, knowing that time and distance have a tendency to ease bad feelings. Just as we do with kids who are in 'brain stem' mode, we can wait for calmer times to have some of those more difficult discussions. Waiting until the conversation can be civil (remember neutralizing arguments?) and productive often makes a world of difference.

Difficult discussions tend to go better when they happen during calm times. Scott found it better to *delay* conversations until all parties were in a controlled state of mind. He found no shame in saying "I do so much better when neither of us is upset or yelling. I'd like to talk about this later. Thanks." It's amazing what a smile and a pleasant tone of voice can do.

We don't have to let our communication deteriorate into fighting and name-calling. We can delay conversations and stay civil when the discussions do take place.

It's hard to measure the value of the messages we send when kids are involved. Too often kids with parents who split get messages that: "adults can't get along," "relationships always go south," and "it's impossible to disagree and still respect each other" rather than hearing messages of resiliency, peace and compromise.

As out-of-control as a breakup can feel, we can still exercise the ultimate control: how we behave. We can choose to be peaceful and respectful in our interactions (and even what we say in the person's absence). We can choose the high road.

And take it from Scott, the high road is a lot less bumpy.

This is powerful stuff! Can you feel it?

I'm particularly excited about sharing this tool with you because it hits most of us right where we live. This tool is the express lane away from chaotic living, and you're going to get excited as you learn to apply this tool to your life.

Living in Chaos

Most of us don't do well with chaos. We appreciate stability, peace and predictability. In fact, we need these qualities in our lives in order to be productive and healthy.

Let's imagine I pick you up at your home, open the door to my car and tell you we're going on a trip.

"Where are we going?" you ask.

"I'm not sure," I say.

I start the engine and begin pulling away from the safety and security of your home.

"How long will we be gone?" you ask.

"I don't know," I respond.

We head toward the freeway.

"You don't know where we're going?" you ask critically.

"No I don't," I responded.

Notice how you're feeling as you receive these answers to your important questions.

"But, you seem to know where you're going," you say, seeking reassurance.

"No, I don't know where I'm going," I say. "But, just sit back and enjoy the ride."

If you are like most of us, you won't enjoy the ride. You want some reassurance that you will be safe. You want to know where you are going and when you will return. More important, you undoubtedly want some input into where you're going and when you will return. To be so out of control is uncomfortable and produces anxiety.

While this scene seems preposterous, many of us often function this way in our life. Many of us are externally controlled, as opposed to being internally controlling of our lives. Instead of setting clear limits on those who might influence our lives, we 'go along for the ride,' with a detrimental impact.

Let's get back to Ariana. Can you see how she is a passenger in her own car? She has gradually let her boyfriend dictate how she is going to live. She hates waiting for him to decide on their relationship, yet that is exactly what she's doing. Her resentment grows hotter by the day, and yet she still does not *offer choices within limits.*

Let's assume she becomes angrier, which is often an emotional clue that our values and boundaries are being violated. (Chaos is another internal cue that something is amiss.) What might she say to offer choices within limits? How about these:

"I care about you very much, and am willing to stay in this relationship as long as you make a commitment to our future within the next sixty days."

"I care about you very much, and am willing to remain social, platonic friends if you cannot commit to marriage within sixty days."

"I care about you very much and am willing to stay in this relationship as long as we attend relationship counseling together to discuss the future of our relationship."

Can you see how Ariana takes back control of her life, while still treating her boyfriend with respect by offering him choices within limits? By taking control of her life she feels a renewed sense of dignity and worth, and eliminates her growing hostility. While she risks losing him, her sense of self-worth is enhanced, enabling her to cope with whatever he decides.

Internal Control

The *Love and Logic* approach honors the ability of every individual to control his or her own life. We believe this is an aspect of personal dignity which simply cannot be ignored or abused in any way. This is why we talk about it as much as we do.

You can see in Ariana's story she did not feel she was in control of her life. In fact, she felt controlled by her boyfriend, and so restoring her sense of dignity must involve her being in control of her life. She must believe she has choices, yet not force her choices on her boyfriend. Just as she must feel in control of her life, her boyfriend has the same needs. When this sense of mutual respect and dignity is out of balance, tension and chaos erupt.

Do either Ariana's story or the "trip in the car" story ring true for your life? Many live in a state of chaos because they have unconsciously given choices for their lives over to others. How does this happen? It happens when we fail to take full responsibility for and control of our lives. There are several key ingredients to taking control of your life. Let's explore some of these critical ingredients.

Assertiveness. Notice Ariana's passivity. She seems almost surprised that she has the right to set boundaries on her boyfriend. However, she feels inept at knowing where and how to set those limits. She has slipped passively into allowing him to dictate the direction of her life, and subsequently feels constant tension and chaos. Understandably so, since she is not in control of her life.

Studies have shown that one of the primary ingredients of a happy life is the feeling that you can determine, in large part, how your life is going. People who feel optimistic about determining the direction of their life, and actively make decisions about their life, feel happy and in control. Those who feel externally directed, by their mate, employer or someone else, feel pessimistic about changing the direction of their life. This often leads to unhappiness.

Our happiness is directly impacted by the degree of control we feel over our life, and the tools in this book are all about taking back control of your life. Assertiveness is a major action used with every other tool we've discussed in this book. Let me offer you a handy definition of assertiveness, sure to guide you in your growth with this tool:

Assertiveness is HARD:

H: *honest*—be honest in your communication with those you care about.

A: *appropriate*—make your communication fit your circumstances.

R: *respectful*—always treat others with respect.

D: *direct*—don't beat around the bush—say it!

Entitlement. What if I told you that you were entitled to determine the direction of your life? What if I said you could be the primary influence regarding the direction of your life? What if you really believed that you could achieve whatever is critically important to you? This belief—that you are *entitled* to determine the direction of your life—would play a huge role in your everyday happiness. And that feeling will come when you master this tool, *offering choices within limits*, added to the other tools provided so far in this book.

Let me say this another way.

Picture your life as a home, with beautiful landscaping, lovely interiors and furnishings that make you feel alive. You've chosen all of this carefully because these things are an expression of who you are, and you're entitled to decorate your life the way you prefer.

Now imagine erecting a lovely boundary—perhaps a stucco wall draped in jasmine, a decorative wrought-iron fence, or some other barrier that states 'this is my space.' Now, imagine a gorgeous gate that swings both open and closed. Imagine that you control that gate, allowing certain people in, and keeping certain people out. Those who enter must behave in accordance with the values important to you.

This is the power and influence you are entitled to in your life. And this gate, both literal and emotional, is the mechanism needed to keep chaos out of your life, and peace, security and predictability in. This is all within your control.

Respect. Assertive, *Love and Logic* communication is always guided by the principle of respect. We always approach an interaction from an I'm okay, you're okay perspective. I want what is best for you as well as being careful to guard what is best for me.

Notice in this type of interaction that neither person has an 'upper hand.' There is no manipulation in order to 'win' over the other, but rather a sense of wanting a healthy interaction. We are able to simultaneously watch over our boundaries while offering choices to the other.

I must warn you that respect of this kind is somewhat addicting. We become used to this kind of interacting very quickly because it feels so good. We notice that others smile when we treat them with respect; they are drawn to us and we are drawn to them.

Responsibility. Do you believe it is your responsibility to effectively manage your life? Not only may you *assertively* manage your life, and are *entitled* to manage your life, but it is your *responsibility* to manage your life. After all, if you don't do it, who will?

Responsibility is made up of two key words: *response* and *ability*. You have the *ability* to *respond* to every situation. You are able to sit back, reflect upon both internal and external cues, and choose how you want to respond. Again, this is your life. This is your Self you must protect and care for. No one else is going to do it—no one!

What will happen if Ariana waits for her boyfriend to decide? We can safely assume she will wait a long time, her resentment and hostility growing by the day. She will feel victimized, worthless, allowing him the power to gradually erode her sense of self-respect. The kicker is, however, her anger will be misdirected. Why? Because it is not his responsibility to protect her. That is her responsibility alone. Giving that power away to others is always a precarious proposition.

Assertiveness, entitlement, respect and *responsibility*—four powerful tools to move you from being externally controlled to being able to effectively *offer choices to others within limits*, thereby taking control of your life and relationships.

My Difficult Boss

"If jobs weren't so hard to find," sulked Will as he walked in the door from work, "I'd quit my job so fast my boss's head would swim. He's a blasted control freak. Every time I come up with a new idea he shoots it down. Everything I suggest is either against policy, or I just get a quick refusal.

"The harder I work to improve the bottom line, the more he pulls rank on me. We can't do anything if it's not his idea. I'm really bummed. I don't even feel like trying anymore."

Will's wife, Jill, was quick with some empathy. "That's got to be so discouraging. I wonder if you could use some laughs?"

"Are you kidding? I'm at the point where I don't know whether to laugh or cry."

"Why don't you tag along with me to my *Love and Logic* parenting class tonight? You'll get some laughs and maybe you'll pick up some new skills. If nothing else, you'll get your mind off of this problem."

Will did have a good time at the class, but better than that, the subject just happened to be about the power of giving choices. As the facilitator went through the rules of giving choices, Will became entranced with the idea of giving two choices you like as opposed to one you like and one you don't. What caught Will's attention was the facilitator's statement that choices are especially effective with strong willed kids, or people with strong control needs.

The facilitator reminded the participants, "Provide your kids two choices, each of which would make you deliriously happy." An example of this might be, "Do you want to wear your coat or just carry it with you?"

Will thought. "I get it. I'd be happy with either choice. My kid's happy because she can feel in control, and the odds of getting in an argument are a lot lower than if I just ordered her to wear her coat."

One of the parents in the group told about an experiment she ran with her little boy. "I have a terrible time getting him to leave the play group. I've made threats, I've bribed him, but every time I tell him it's time to leave, he throws a fit.

"Yesterday, ten minutes before it was time to leave, I said to him, 'Toby. Do you want to leave right now, or do want to do it in ten minutes? It's up to you.' To my amazement, he said, 'Ten minutes, Mommy.' "

"I couldn't believe it, but ten minutes later I told him the ten minutes were up and it was time to leave. This was the first time we left without a problem. It was so simple. Now I'm going to think up a lot of different ways to use this technique."

Will left the class with a new view of the problem with his boss. "You know, Jill. That *Love and Logic* facilitator was really talking about my boss tonight. My boss has some intense control needs. I wonder if I've been approaching things the wrong way?

"I've been giving my boss one choice and one choice only each time I make a suggestion. I bet he gets his control needs met by rejecting my idea. I wonder what would happen if I approached him with two choices each time. I'm going to figure out how to offer two different ideas next time, either one I'd be happy with."

It wasn't long before Will had a chance to run his experiment. Entering the boss's office Will said, "Boss, I've got this problem to solve. I've got two proposals here. Would you rather read them or have me tell you about them?"

Will's boss was quick to say, "Just tell me about them." (The boss still felt that he was in control. It's difficult to say no to two different choices.)

After explaining the two proposals, Will asked, "Which one do you think I ought to do?"

Without missing a beat his boss got his control needs met by answering, "Better go with the first one. Let's get this problem solved as soon as possible. Thanks, Will."

Will arrived home in higher spirits that evening. His needs to feel effective had been met, while at the same time his boss's control needs had been satisfied. The boss didn't have to say, "No," just to feel in control.

Studies in control theory tell us that the stronger a person's control needs are, the quicker they are to jump on the opportunity to make choices. It also tells us that the more insecure a person is, the more effective they feel when offered choices. It is often easier to recognize an offered solution than it is to create one on our own.

Getting back to Will's boss, he had probably found it easier to say, "No," in the past, than to have to create solutions. This, combined with his strong control needs might explain why he often rejected ideas based upon following policy.

Will solved several problems with one simple technique, *offering choices*.

Mutually Offering Choices

My guess is that by now some of you are squirming at the thought of offering others choices, as if you were given some magical power. Many are incredibly uncomfortable when they speak with their big boy/big girl voice, telling others how to behave if they want to enter your garden.

I want to remind you, however, that the same power you have, they have. The same response-ability you now have is the same response-ability they have. This is not a one-sided sense of power, but rather a *mutual* sense of power with plenty of opportunity for give and take, and mutual respect.

This sense of mutual choice-making was driven home to me the other day when a neighbor of mine, Roberto, came over to talk to me.

"David," he said in a rather stern voice, "I've been meaning to talk to you."

"What is it?" I asked.

"I cannot have your guests park in my driveway when they come over to your house. This has happened more than once and I haven't said anything. But, it happened again last evening and I cannot allow it to happen any more unless you make prior arrangements with me.

If you talk to me first I'm sure we can figure out where your guests can park so as not to disrupt my coming and going."

"Thanks for telling me, Roberto," I said. "I wasn't aware this was happening and I should have paid closer attention. I won't let it happen again and will certainly talk to you first if I need extra parking."

"Thank you very much," he said, "and have fun."

Roberto walked away, waving as he left.

There was a time when I felt uncomfortable with such an encounter. I would have felt guilty and awkward, probably even slightly annoyed. Practicing assertiveness, however, has given me a sense of self-confidence. I'm able to see the other's point of view and empathize with his or her position. I'm able to hear another's concern while maintaining my sense of dignity.

Reflecting upon Roberto's approach, I felt encouraged that he was comfortable enough with me to approach me with his concern. Furthermore, I appreciated that he offered me some choice in the matter—that if I approached him ahead of time, we could find a way to meet both of our needs.

Our interaction was Honest, Appropriate, Respectful and Direct—all the ingredients of an assertive encounter. The air was cleared and we were now free to enjoy a friendly, neighborly relationship.

Limits

Throughout this book we've emphasized the power and importance of limits, both in how we communicate and what we will tolerate from others. Limits are absolutely necessary to inform us and others how we will communicate.

Limits also serve as forms of *protection*. Anything we value has limits/boundaries placed around it. Whether it comes to something as practical as our home, vehicle, personal belongings, or aspects of our Self, we protect it—or at least we should. We create literal or emotional fences around it to ensure its safety.

Limits also provide a sense of predictability. When I see or hear about fences/limits, I know what I can expect to happen in any given situation. I know how to navigate in an area with limits and boundaries.

When using the *Love and Logic* approach with children we say things like, "Feel free to stay up until 9 tonight as long as your homework is finished." Such a simple statement gives a powerful message to children. They have the response-ability to watch their favorite evening television program with the condition that their homework is done. *Offering choices within limits.* (We might also add enforceable consequences!)

When using this same tool with adults we give definable limits—the area within which we will relate to each other: "I'm very willing to spend the weekend with your parents as long as we have time in the evenings to be alone together."

Can you see how clear and empowering this statement is? We proclaim a willingness to participate in something of value to our mate as long as our boundaries are respected in return. (My need to spend quality, alone time with him/her.)

We might also add something like this: "If you would rather visit your parents alone, that would also be all right with me. Perhaps we can spend the evening together before you go."

Notice all the possibilities. Notice how well I am taking care of myself while also being sensitive to what my mate may need. These principles are never meant to be "all about me," but rather taking care of *us.* We firmly believe that when we take care of *us,* we will take care of both you and me!

Freedom

"Go outside and play," my mother used to say, "but don't leave the neighborhood."

I knew exactly what she meant. I knew that I was allowed to play two houses down in both directions, *but no further.* I knew that if I followed her instructions I'd be allowed to play freely. If I pushed the limits, however, I'd be grounded to the house—something I found intolerable.

Using *Love and Logic* language she would have said, "Feel free to play with your friends as long as you stay within two houses of ours. You can choose to play one or two houses from ours in either direction, or else we'll need to talk about this agreement." (I figured out what she was hinting at when she said that!)

Limits, in this case, offered me freedom. My mother offered clear expectations which were quite tolerable to me. Knowing exactly where I stood allowed me to make choices, increasing my sense of independence and self-esteem. Testing the limits allowed me to learn that boundaries were to be respected—an invaluable lesson.

Fences, boundaries, gates and limits all spell two things: *freedom* and *responsibility*. The more often we are responsible, the more freedom we are allowed. This principle was true as a child and is equally true as an adult.

This same sense of freedom is available to us as adults. As I define what works for me and what doesn't, and let others know this, I am able to relate to them from a healthy place of freedom. When I violate my own boundaries, or allow others to violate them, bitterness creeps in, and that is something none of us want in our relationships.

Can you see the importance of limits? Do you see how limits are directly tied to freedom? Can you imagine practicing using them in your life? Let's see how you apply these tools in a practical way to your life.

Run This Experiment

You can see our tools all involve insisting upon respect for yourself and others. They reinforce assertiveness, limits, and choices, all leading to personal strength and freedom. These tools all fit powerfully together.

Now it's time to practice this latest tool: *offering choices within limits* with some significant person in your life. Choose someone you have a close relationship with. Give consideration to something of importance to you, perhaps something you need from them. Try offering them a choice with a limit attached.

Love and Logic Magic for Lasting Relationships

Here are some ideas:

- I'll be happy to meet you for lunch if you are prompt.
- I'd love to spend more time with you as long as you give me your undivided attention.
- We'll enjoy a livelier sexual relationship if you take me out on dates more frequently.

Now you try it. Remember, it's okay to feel a bit awkward as you try this. We expect you to try, test, tweak and try again. It's okay if things don't work perfectly. See how the tool might best fit into your particular situation.

Are you're gaining self-confidence as you practice these tools? They are powerful and will make an incredible difference in your relationships. And we still have one more super-powerful tool to put in your toolbox: *Catching them doing it right*.

CHAPTER NINE

9

Catching Them
Doing It Right

*"Go confidently in the direction of your dreams.
Live the life you have imagined."*

—HENRY DAVID THOREAU

The folks at the *Love and Logic Institute* figured out something right off
the bat that transformed the way teachers interacted with students.
They discovered that criticism just doesn't work. Criticism is the fastest
way to get someone to react from their brainstem, creating instant war.

The same principle is true for adults. Criticize me and I'm not going
to like you, at the least, and there's a good chance it will go from bad
to worse. Chances are excellent not only will I not like you, but I'll
probably get hooked and fire something back at you that you won't
like—and then neither of us will be real happy with the end result.

So, my brainstem functioning (criticism) hooks your brainstem
functioning (defensive rebuttal) and we're off to the races. There
has to be a better way, and thank goodness we found it.

It's called *encouragement.*

This stuff is not new. Grandma said it like this: "You catch more
flys with honey than vinegar." How right she was.

Scientists have now proven her words to be true. Encouragement changes behavior far more effectively than discouragement or criticism. In fact, criticism causes people to rebel against us, often doing the very thing they ask us not to do.

Encouragment, on the other hand, hooks the frontal lobe, the planning part of our brains. We want to cooperate with someone we know cares about us and has our best interests at heart. We work hard for teachers who empathize with us, and strive to please those adults in our world who tune into our feelings and offer us encouragement.

This point comes alive for me every week at my piano lesson. I have started piano lessons again after a brief (fifty year) hiatus. Needless to say, I've forgotten anything I learned when I was nine years old. I'm now asking my older brain to convince my fingers to move up and down the keyboard in awkward motions making something akin to music. My fingers don't always cooperate. But—and this is important—Trish, my teacher, is always there to tell me I can do it.

The truth of the matter is, I can't always do exactly what the lesson calls for. However, in her ingenious way of teaching, if I can't do it exactly the way the lesson calls for, she breaks down the lesson into smaller bites, creating ways for me to succeed. She knows that success is the best breeder of future success. Encouragement is her primary tool—and it works. She is a perfect example of someone who has already mastered this final tool: *catching them doing it right*. I'm still taking lessons!

The Old Way

Jim Fay loves to tell the story of the teacher who, out of pure frustration, forgets everything she learned about the *Love and Logic* approach. This teacher forgot that we always:

- Share control
- Show respect and dignity
- Set enforceable consequences
- Provide empathy/consequence formulas
- Offer choices with limits

This teacher, unprepared and generally annoyed at her student, yelled, "You better stop acting this way or you're going to the principal's office."

The student is not frightened by this threat and, in fact, doubts the teacher will even follow through with it.

"I don't care," the student hollers back, fully engaged in brainstem functioning.

"Well you will care when you're sitting with Mr. Johnson," she says, also fully in brainstem mode.

"I doubt it," he says.

"Go down to the office, right now," she says screaming.

He mutters some obscenities and heads for the office.

Jim asks the question:

"Did the teacher follow the *Love and Logic* principles? Of course not. Did the student learn anything, besides how much he dislikes this teacher? Not likely. Will her actions help this student learn more in the future? Not all all."

Before we become too critical of this teacher, we know what it is like to function from our brainstem as opposed to having gone through a planning session so we know how we're going to act when faced with such a situation. (And we're all going to face someone, at some time, and be tempted to react instead of act.)

I distinctly recall reacting critically with my wife, Christie. She had gotten home half an hour late without calling and you'd think she'd robbed the Bank of America by the way I reacted.

Cornering her in the kitchen, I began my interrogation.

"Where have you been? Why are you so late?" I asked.

"I don't know," she said, taken by surprise at the intensity of my questioning. "What's the big deal?"

"Well, I was expecting you nearly an hour ago, and you didn't even call," I said abruptly, feeling a false sense of righteous indignation.

At this point Christie began to be annoyed at me for my controlling behavior.

"Geez, I'm sorry," she shot back at me. "Why are you so upset?" (Good question!)

"I'm upset because you're late. That's why. You could have had the courtesy to call."

Much like the student in the previous section, Christie muttered something at me and walked away.

What had I gained in this interation? Nothing, except for one angry wife. Did she learn anything, besides how angry she was at me? No. Could I have handled this scene much better? Yes.

These kinds of reactive functioning can be, for all of us, a thing of our past. We now know about *treating others with dignity, setting enforceable limits, sharing control of the problem and offering choices within limits.* And now we're adding to these tools another powerful tool: *catching them doing it right.*

Subtleties of The Old Way

These examples of *doing it wrong* are over-the-top wrong, and we all know it. It won't take a great deal of change to eliminate them from our behavior repertoire. These overreactions are *so wrong*, it's not Rocket Science to realize we must eliminate them from our behavior. But, what about subtle tactics we use to convey criticism?

The tricky part often comes from subtle aspects of *the old way.* What I mean here is that many people give up the global, large-scale aspects of criticism, while never changing subtleties of critical behavior. Consider these routines aspects of criticism we might use:

Shaming another for something they've done wrong.
Ridiculing another's behavior.
Judging another's actions.
Judging another's intentions.
Reading another's mind. (Impossible to do, by the way!)

Most of us are hyper-alert to feeling judged, having been ridiculed as a child. Sensing anything similar to judgment as an adult sets off a red-alert alarm inside our brain indicating "fight or flight." In any situation involving feeling shamed we're likely to take drastic action, though our mate may not even know what happened. The culprit is almost always *shame*.

Consider the following example:

A middle-aged couple came to see me recently because their marriage was ready to dissolve. He had initiated contact with me because he had been having an affair and ended it in order to give his marriage "one last chance." Before working with them as a couple I asked to spend time with him individually.

"Why did you have the affair, Will?" I asked. "What do you think you got from the other woman that you couldn't get from your wife?"

"That's easy," he said confidently. "Kelly likes me. She makes me feel good. My wife just seems to tolerate me. She is always critical of me in subtle ways. She doesn't even know she's doing it, and when I call her attention to it she gets mad at me. Here she is the one putting me down, and when I call it to her attention, she gets madder. So, I gave up."

"And found someone who doesn't put you down."

"Pretty much," Will said. "Look. I didn't go after this woman, but when you're not getting any encouragement at home, I bet a lot of people would do what I did."

"Let's talk about the criticism you feel from your wife," I said.

Will paused, becoming noticeably saddened.

"She doesn't even know she's doing it," Will said. "She criticizes me for the friends I choose, the way I dress, even the way I do my job. A man wants to be respected, and while I think she loves me, I'm not sure she respects me."

Will stopped for a moment and then continued.

"How would you feel if your wife said these things to you:

- *"Why are your friends always taking advantage of you?"*
- *"Why don't you grow a beard. You look better in a beard."*
- *"You need to talk to your boss about the way the company treats you. You let them use you."*

- *"You need to stand up for yourself with people."*

"What she doesn't realize is that these comments stick to me. I don't forget about them. They run through my mind all day long. I wonder if I'll ever be able to be enough for her."

"I sense a lot of hurt, Will," I said.

"And now you know how I could do something I don't believe in—have an affair. I want my marriage to work, but I'm desperate for someone who believes in me."

While I was certainly concerned about the condition of their marriage, I knew I could help them with some *Love and Logic* tools. Both were motivated to save their marriage, and that's usually all I need to get couples from a tough place to a much smoother way of relating. While it was painful to talk about the affair, it opened the door to talk about relating in a new way—one filled with encouragement and respect. Both agreed to work toward eliminating brainstem relating from their communication and replace it with *catching each other doing things right.*

The New Way

Thank goodness there are new ways of interacting. We're never stuck in old ways of doing things that don't work. This book is chock full of new tools, each of which build on the others to create a powerful box of tools.

Are you feeling empowered? Are you excited as you run your experiments, finding which tools fit you best?

So, the old way is: *get mad, lose control, operate reactively from brainstem functioning, and pray like crazy that something gets through to the other person—which it won't.*

Now, the new way.

Fully prepared, with responses rehearsed so that you feel self-confident, you watch for opportunities to *catch them doing things right.*

What exactly does this mean? It means that you have already offered them choices within limits, and then you watch closely for a chance to say something like this:

"Thank you so much for setting aside time for us tonight. I feel really close to you when you make such an effort to be close to me."

"I really appreciate the efforts you make for me, like when you went out of your way to get the coffee ready for me in the morning. That means so much to me."

"I am lucky to be with such a thoughtful person who plans ahead for special evenings out."

"Thank you for coming to me and talking directly with me about concerns you have for our relationship."

Notice that in each example I conveyed several things:

1. How I felt.
2. How I felt about something specific the other person did.
3. How I conveyed the impact their behavior would likely have upon me, giving them ideas about what they might want to do in the future. (Assuming they want an intimate, loving and exciting relationship.)

These examples of interaction are ways to increase specific behaviors. And remember, if we want a particular behavior to increase, *we offer encouragement, not criticism*. Let's explore in more depth why encouragement makes such a potent impact.

The Power of Encouragement

We all know there is tremendous power in encouragement. We've learned in recent years that students who are encouraged to perform at a higher level do so. Those who are discouraged and doubt themselves often slip into the depths of a self-fulfilling prophecy.

It's been said, "Whether you think you can, or can't, you're right."

This is the power of encouragment and self-belief, and self-confidence is impacted tremendously by those around us offering encouragement.

My associate, Chuck, decided later in life (in his late fifties) that he wanted to leave the radio business in pursuit of a counseling degree. While he had achieved the pinnacle of success as a broadcaster, he always wanted to help others more personally, and felt he had the personality to do so.

As he tells it, "I knew I was nearly sixty years old and it was now or never. Lots of people questioned my decision, but I had one person who really encouraged me. Julie (his girlfriend) told me that if this was something I wanted to do, go for it. You're going to get older anyway, so why not get older doing something you really want to do. That was all the encouragement I needed."

Nearly half way through the program Chuck asked if I would serve as a Supervisor for an internship. With boundless enthusiasm, excited about diving into counseling, we teamed up.

But that is not the end of the story.

Half way through his second year the doctors discovered a cancerous tumor on his thyroid gland. Having conquered cancer twenty years earlier, I've watched him face this serious threat to his health with aplomb.

"I've got too much to do to let this slow me down," he said confidently.

Stunned by his courage and tenacity, I asked questions about where he gets the strength to face these challenges.

"Julie encourages me," he says smiling. "She catches me doing things right in our relationship and that gives me the gas I need to keep going."

Still gushing with excitement, he added, "Julie notices my excitement about counseling. She comments on the papers I'm writing and the energy I get from working with people. When I get discouraged, she picks me up, reminding me that what I'm doing is a good fit for me."

I watch Chuck and remind myself of the importance of encouragement—and the power of being caught doing it right.

Mutual Admiration Society

Listening to Chuck talk about the encouragement he receives from his girlfriend, Julie, tells a powerful story. There is a reverberating effect that occurs when we encourage each other. I call it the *Mutual Admiration Society*. The rules for this club are simple:

> *You encourage me, and I encourage you. I feel so good by your encouragement that I naturally want to encourage you. I see what brings joy to your life and I want that for you. You see what brings joy to my life and you want that for me. We create an environment where joy and encouragement naturally flourish.*
> *We maintain a positive focus at all times.*

Can you imagine such a world? Can you imagine taking an active role in creating such a society with your loved ones? This world is available to you and me at any time, simply by making a choice. We must choose to let go of old ways of interacting, never allowing ourselves to slip into petty criticisms, sarcasm or anger. We form an invisible barrier to these toxic conditions, and fiercely guard our little society.

The more we practice thinking positive thoughts and guard our actions, the more we feel uncomfortable being critical. Funny how that works. It is as if we are creating a special place within ourselves where only good thoughts and attitudes can reside. When other uglier feelings and thoughts creep in, we treat them as unwelcome visitors.

We have witnessed first hand the power of encouragement and positive thoughts. Imagine a pebble thrown into a pond. The ripples extend indefinitely. Imagine now that the pebble thrown into the pond is a positive statement of encouragement for your mate and loved ones. Imagine this pebble of positivity thrown into the pond for everyone in your world.

My wife, Christie, and I have made a pact in recent years to eliminate criticism and judgments from our vocabulary. I cannot say that we don't slip from time to time, but when we do one of us gently reminds the other that we don't want a world of judging others. Admiring those in our world feels so good that we no longer like the feeling that comes from putting others down.

Unrealistic, you say? I don't think so. Hard, yes. Unrealistic, no. We choose every day to guard how we think and what we say about others. We begin with our marriage and move out from there. We spread our good will to our family and friends, and even to the clerk at the local store. We are non-verbally inviting everyone into our Mutual Admiration Society. Do you want to join?

Between Dishes and Dandelions

Remember, we like to keep things simple, and I want to encourage you in making changes regarding encouragement. Making changes in the way you communicate—*catching them doing it right*—will occur in everyday situations, from catching your wife doing the dishes to catching him mowing the lawn.

We're not talking about profound changes—simple things that all add up. If you catch him doing the dishes, and emphasize your appreciation of that, chances are you'll also catch her when she goes out of her way to make your favorite meal. If you thank him for keeping the lawn mowed and edged, chances are you'll also thank him for working so hard at his job for the family.

And, chances are all of these actions will add up. One small word of encouragement here, one thank you there, and an 'atta boy' surprise. These are the little things that take an average relationship and make it great.

Now, can you imagine yourself making these small changes? Nothing earth shattering. Small, day to day observations and comments that change the tone of your home. Don't for a moment think that dishes and dandelions can't make a difference, because they can—and do.

Run This Experiment

We're approaching the end of the book, the super finale. We've only got one more small chapter to pull things together, but you have still have a chance to run another experiment.

This one is one of the easiest. It's your chance to catch your mate, or some other significant person in your life, doing it right. Take a few moments and consider what you appreciate about what this special person does for you. What would you like to reinforce by noticing it and offering encouragement? What quality do you particularly appreciate that you want to reinforce? Perhaps it is not a quality at all, but rather something they do that brings a smile to your face. Encourage it.

If you're still at a loss for what to do, let me offer a few suggestions:

1. Offer a positive comment on something your mate does that you appreciate.
2. Compliment your mate for the way he or she dresses.
3. Notice something your mate struggles with where a word of encouragement might bring him or her hope.
4. Notice a trait your mate has been trying to change, and comment when he or she does it more effectively.
5. Compliment your mate for tenacity or courage he or she exhibits in his or her life.

As always, try it, test it and then tweak it. This is all One Big Experiment, where you get to decide what works and what doesn't.

We've reached the Close To The End section of this book. We're impressed that you've worked as hard as you have on learning these new strategies for making your relationship work. We hope you've found the excitement so many others have found, and have witnessed first hand the power of the *Love and Logic* approach to get along.

Epilogue

*"The best day of your life is the one on which you decide your life is
your own. No apologies or excuses. No one to lean on, rely on, or
blame. The gift is yours—it is an amazing journey—and you alone are
responsible for the quality of it. This is the day your life really begins."*

—BOB MOAWAD

Okay, here we are at the end of the book. We have journeyed
together through many situations, complications and challenges.
Each step of the way we've introduced a new, powerful tool that
can transform problems into opportunities.

Remember, no step in life is wasted. You have a wealth of experience under your belt, with each new situation you encounter ready
to teach you something important. You have seen how the old way
of doing things simply doesn't work, and throughout the book you've
practiced new tools, able to greatly improve your relationships.

Today you complete Flight Instruction and are ready for your
first solo flight. But, don't worry. You're ready. Besides, it's really
not that hard. All you have to do is try, test, tweak and try again.
That formula never fails.

Whether you approached this book from a place where you simply wanted to make your life better, or desperately needed help, *Love and Logic Magic for Lasting Relationships* guides you through the steps to get you where you want to go.

We make few grandiose claims about the tools in this book, though we do make one: *one or more of these tools is going to fit you like a glove.* We never know which one (or more) is going to do the trick, but we've been at this long enough to see people latch onto at least one tool and use it to bring order and harmony to their relationships.

Just yesterday a woman called to *create a planning session* where she planned to enforce some boundaries with her boss. She wanted to make sure—which was a good thing!—she was really ready to let him know his angry tirades were intolerable, and he could expect certain actions from *her* if he blew up at her again. Lack of preparation is where things sometimes fall apart, so I was particularly excited she wanted to prepare for any possibility.

Together we walked through the problem—his angry outbursts—and her options, which were many. We discussed what she could impact, and what she couldn't. She wanted to make sure she had her *enforceable consequences* ready, knowing that if she offered empty threats she would be in for a bad time.

I've not heard how it all worked out for her, but I'm certain of one thing: *she's confident, ready and beginning to change, and you can be sure her husband is taking notice.* Remember, when one person in a relationship begins acting differently, everyone notices! Like a mobile, when you move any piece of the mobile, every other piece must necessarily feel the impact. This is our promise to you as well.

Dispelling a Myth

There is a myth I must dispel before we come to the end of our book. Here it is: *You can't change anyone else.* Now I must admit I'm being a little tricky with you. While it is certainly true we cannot directly change another person, consider the following scenarios and tell me if the other person will be impacted:

SCENE ONE: A woman informs her boss she will no longer tolerate his yelling. She tells him he is free to continue yelling, but she is prepared to talk to Human Resources if it continues.

SCENE TWO: A man informs his friend he will no longer tolerate his drinking. He tells him he is free to drink, but he will no longer join him in public or join him at his home if he chooses to do so.

SCENE THREE: A man and woman sit down together to talk about their fighting. Both agree if either of them use foul language with the other, the violator will leave the house for the evening and cannot return until he/she has used the Three A's (Apology, Accepting Responsibility, Appropriate Amends) and both agree he/she is ready to return home.

SCENE FOUR: A sister informs her brother she will no longer tolerate his ridiculing behavior. She makes it clear she won't visit him again, or invite him to visit, if he treats her with sarcasm or disrespect.

Notice in each of these situations there is no grand gesturing or idle threats. There is no screaming or throwing temper tantrums. In each situation the individuals have prepared ahead of time for the encounter. They know exactly what they will do *if* the other behaves in a certain way. Each is determined to treat the other with complete respect, honoring the other's right to choose whatever they like. While the other is completely free to act in any way they choose, the user of the *Love and Logic* tools is in complete control of what *they* will do—*and their behavior will have a profound impact on the other.*

So, can a teacher make a student behave? Not by force, intimidation and empty threats. They can, however, create an environment where student behavior is predictably controlled. Can you make your spouse act in a more responsible manner? Can you make your sibling or aging parent treat you with respect? Not directly. *But, using the empathy/ consequences formula, planned strategy* sessions and setting limits with enforceable consequences, we can set things up so the system will change—thereby changing the individuals involved.

Said simply, you've got a lot of power! Use it wisely.

Selling Confidence

Writing about Love and Logic techniques with adults has reminded me of their inherent power to not only transform a relationship into a better one, but to create self-confidence in the user of those techniques. We like selling self-confidence, because when you are self-confident you are more likely not only to follow through with the tools, but will do so with more authority.

Now we're not talking authority in the sense of bossing anyone around. Quite the contrary. Remember, we share control over every situation. We're in this together with our mate, family and friends. We remind ourselves there are no wrong choices, and every situation brings a new opportunity for growth. We hold our heads high with the knowledge we have a pretty good idea of how we're going to handle a particular situation. Even when we aren't exactly certain of our next step, we're certain we can take the necessary time and space to plan our next step—and that breeds confidence.

You are now armed with many power-packed tools, and the knowledge of how to use them. Can you feel a little extra spring in your step? Are you itching to use more of these tools? Like Clint Eastwood, you're tempted to say to someone who mistreats you, "Go ahead. Make my day."

I'm only half-serious here, because we're also completely dedicated to treating everyone with respect. So, even if someone mistreats you, you'll never mistreat them. You will, however, let them know things are about to change, and this always commands respect.

So, take a deep breath, relax, and puff out your chest ever-so-slightly with the knowledge you are much better equipped to face any relationship problem. If ever in doubt, simply look back through the book and you'll find the answers you need, an experiment to try.

The Love and Logic Way

In addition to giving you just a bit of new information to top off your toolbox, the Epilogue is always a great place to remind readers of what they've read.

So, in keeping with Excellent Epilogue Writing, let me remind you of the *Four Basic Tenets*, which must be part of everything you do. These principles form the foundation for all the tools we've offered in the book. Jim Fay and Foster Cline say everything flows out of these four important principles:

1. **We always maintain the dignity of individuals:** Everyone desires to be treated with dignity. There is never a need to shame or disrespect another person.

2. **We share control:** We share control over how we're going to solve problems. We understand you control your feelings and actions, I control my feelings and actions, and we control our relationship. Control is such a strong basic need that the more we share the more we get back.

3. **We share the thinking:** It is up to us to think about our problems. We negotiate with one another over the direction of our relationship. Asking for another's thoughts provides dignity, enhances relationships, and shares control.

4. **We follow an empathy/ consequence formula:** We work together to develop healthy boundaries, and understand empathy is the glue that holds us together. Providing empathy for the other's problems instead of telling them what to do provides dignity, shares the thinking, shares control, and enhances relationships.

Wrapped in these principles you can see we never overwhelm others with intimidation. We are able to be cool, calm and collected because we've planned ahead how we're going to behave in a given situation.

Using these principles, we do not assume a person is going to act just the way we want them to. They're free to act any way they'd like. While there will be repercussions for any of their choices, we allow them the dignity to choose their actions and take responsibility for the consequences of them.

You'll notice that we also want to facilitate a team-building atmosphere, always asking questions like, "How do you think we should handle this situation? Since I can't tolerate X, and you seem to want to behave Y, I'm not sure what to do. What do you think?" Asking for input offers dignity to others and alerts them to the fact we're thinking long and hard about the problem, and we *are going to take some kind of action.*

The old ways of doing things aren't working, and we're putting the people in our world on notice that *things are going to change, one way or another.* (And remember, we don't even need to know what we're going to do.)

Embracing Mistakes

Another important principle you must keep in mind is *mistakes are our friends.* Mistakes teach us what doesn't work. Making small mistakes stops us from making larger mistakes.

You have learned the importance of leaning into your mistakes. Rather than being frightened of mistakes, you've learned to embrace mistakes, gleaning from them every possible ounce of wisdom they contain. Like messages written in code, your job is to pick them up, hold them to the light, turn them over in your hands, and feel them. What is their message? How have they come to help you?

Those unfamiliar with the *Love and Logic* approach are either paralyzed by mistakes, or shame others for making them. We know better. Rather than being paralyzed by mistakes, we greet them with humility. In a rather Zen-like way, we bow to them. We allow ourselves, our mates, our friends and our children to make them without making a big deal about it. Why? *Because mistakes are a great opportunity for learning.*

So, have you learned to be comfortable with your mistakes? Can you sit back and smile after making a doozy?

One of the first things I tell couples who come to work with me is:

"You have come to see me because you are making a lot of mistakes. It's okay, because you don't know better. I applaud your courage to come and work with me, and together we'll look closely at your relationship and see where you're making mistakes. Then, when we identify exactly which mistakes you're making over and over again, we will talk about new behaviors you can use to make your relationships work much more smoothly."

After letting my words sink in, I ask this question.

"How would you feel if I looked at you and said, 'I don't see anything you're doing wrong. I don't think you need to see someone like me.'"

Of course they would be shocked and undoubtedly ask for their money back. They know what they're doing isn't working, and want someone to point out exactly what that is. Pretending there is nothing wrong, or we don't need help is like having a medical problem and ignoring it. Not smart.

Since you've made it this far in the book I assume you know you need to change some things—and now you're armed with a box full of tools to make those changes. Give them a try, they work!

Empowered

I couldn't wait to write this book with Jim Fay. It's not every day a small-town psychologist who has been using the *Love and Logic* approach gets to write with the top dog. Starting as half a lark, a long-distance phone call and an opportune meeting in Portland, Oregon, a book is now complete. Not just any book, but a book packed with opportunities.

So, like the Cheshire Cat, I'm smiling. I was handed a box of powerful tools being used by thousands of parents and educators and told I could shape-shift them slightly to be used by another audience. It didn't take much work. Just a lovely visit to Jim and Shirley's home in Colorado, a bunch of phone calls back and forth, listening to Jim's throaty laugh, and hearing story after story of successes with these tools. Not a bad gig if you can get it—and I did!

So, you're holding a box of tools. Remember, however, that tools left in a tool box are of little use. Each one holds incredible power, but to benefit from them, you *must* take them out and use them. I promise if you do, you'll be pleased. Jim would like that too!

Let's Keep Experimenting with Getting Along

Thank you for reading this book. Thank you for embracing the tools we are indebted to Jim Fay and Foster Cline for developing. These tools have worked for thousands of teachers and parents, and we knew it was just a matter of time before they were applied to everyone in a relationship. And that includes everyone on this planet.

So, continuing with a playful attitude and a curious spirit, let's keep experimenting with getting along.

About the Authors:

Jim Fay—
Jim Fay is one of America's most sought-after presenters and authors in the area of parenting and school discipline. His background includes 31 years as a teacher and administrator, over three decades as a professional consultant, and many years as the parent of three children. Jim's sense of humor and infectious spirit have made his interviews, audios, videos, and books popular with educators and parents as well as the national news media. Jim has discovered that fun stories are the most powerful way of helping people learn. He often comments, "People seem to learn best when they giggle." You will find this delightful quality in many of our Love and Logic products.

Dr. David B. Hawkins—
Dr. David has been counseling for over thirty years, helping people discover ways to overcome obstacles on their journey to happiness. He enjoys working with couples, assisting them to rise above challenges as they seek more satisfying and fulfilling relationships. His strengths include helping individuals understand issues that disrupt their lives, and finding ways to grow beyond them. He is the author of over thirty books, including the best-sellers *When Pleasing Others is Hurting You* and *Dealing With the CrazyMakers in Your Life*. He is the advice columnist for Crosswalk.com and CBN.org, is a weekly guest on Moody Radio and has been on numerous national television shows promoting his books. He has shared the *Love and Logic* approach, and is a national speaker for counseling organizations. He lived last summer with his wife, Christie, an Interior Designer, on their sailboat and now they make their home on Bainbridge Island, Washington.

Jim Fay presents *Love and Logic* seminars for both parents and educators in many cities each year. For more information on other books, CDs, DVDs and seminars, call us today to find the right *Love and Logic* solutions geared product for you! 800-338-4065 or visit www.loveandlogic.com

Dr. Hawkins is available for speaking engagements, showing you how you can apply *Love and Logic* strategies to your business, church, personal, friendship and work relationships. He has designed three-hour workshops to fit every situation. To schedule a speaking engagement, contact him through his personal website, YourRelationshipDoctor.com, yourrelationshipdoctor@yahoo.com or call him at 360-490-5446.

Index: